The PATHWAY *to* PEACE *and* JOY

"*I AM*" the *Rose of Sharon*" (*Song of Solomon* 2:1).

Amy E. Socha R.N.

ISBN 979-8-88685-541-8 (paperback)
ISBN 979-8-88685-542-5 (digital)

Christian Faith Publishing
832 Park Avenue
Meadville, PA 16335
www.christianfaithpublishing.com

Printed in the United States of America

Acknowledgments

I wish to express my deep appreciation for all the help, input, and encouragement of various pastors, such as Pastor Ferdinand O. Bahr, Reverend Richard Ames, Reverend Paul Eggold, Reverend David York, Pastor Mark Smith, and Reverend Kevin Parviz. Also very helpful were the directors of several Evangelism to the Jews organizations, among whom are David Brickner from Jews for Jesus, Steve Cohan and Alan Butterworth from Apple of His Eye ministry to the Jews, and Reverend Kevin Parviz from Burning Bush ministry to the Jews. In addition, several employees of these organizations, such as Mrs. Marty Walker and Ruth Rosen from Jews for Jesus and former employee of Apple of His Eye, Kimberly Mallegni. Included are the entire staff of Christian Faith Publishing, especially literary agent Marie Lewis, and my three publication specialists, Mary Jones, Jordyn Funkhauser, and Megan Andrews. Last but not least, my wonderful husband, Arthur; sister-in-law, Nancy Roets (who suggested the Shalom [meaning peace] at the end of the book); my brother, David Schmidtke; my cousins, Steven Schmidtke and Carl Mueller; my friends, Harvey Kaplan, Richard Thompson, Greg Steele, author John Lundstrom, Bob Rothwell, Doralene Zunker, my friend since grade school; and all my other wonderful relatives and friends. May God bless them all for their input and encouragement!

The Pathway to *Peace* and *Joy*

Do you want to be absolutely <u>sure</u> that you will have *peace* and *joy* in this life and that you are on the *pathway* leading to *perfect, everlasting joy* and *peace* in heaven? Then this book is for you. After all, *Jesus* said, "For what is a man profited, if he shall gain the whole world, and lose his own soul?" (*Matthew* 16:26).

 God has *revealed* to you how you can have <u>complete</u> <u>assurance</u> of both earthly and heavenly *peace* and *joy*!

Chapter 1

I have good news for you! *God truly does exist!* What is even better is that *He* loves you and longs for an intimate, trusting, personal relationship with you! *He* loves you because *He* created you and wants you to really get to know *Him. He* wants you to be able to have *His best*—a peaceful and joyful life here on earth and the most *peaceful* and *joyful* life possible in eternity (forever and ever).

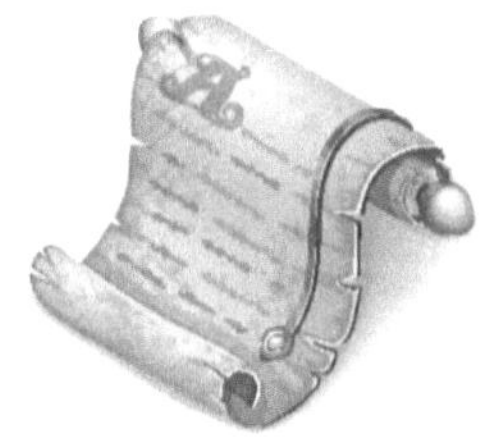

God wanted to communicate with us somehow. What better means could *He* have chosen to tell us about *Himself* than the written *Word* revealed through the *ancient* writings of the *Old* and *New Testament Scriptures?* The name ascribed to the *Old Testament Scriptures* is the *Tanakh*. It was written approximately three thousand years ago. Copies of the original *Tanakh* were found in the *Dead Sea Scrolls*. From 1947 to 1956, these manuscripts were discovered in eleven caves in and around the ruins of an *ancient* city called Khirbet Qumran in the country of Israel. More *ancient* manuscripts were later discovered in the Middle East, and these *New Testament* works were written by some of the original twelve disciples (followers) and other avid and devout believers in *Jesus Christ*.

The book of *2 Peter* describes many of these *writers* as actual *"eyewitnesses of His Majesty"* (*2 Peter* 1:16). Many became faithful missionaries to foreign lands, who would suffer death rather than deny their *Lord* and *Savior*. Would you be willing to die for something you knew to be false and didn't really believe in? I seriously doubt it! In that same chapter of *Peter's book*, it is revealed that *"no prophecy of the Scripture is of any private interpretation. For the prophecy came not in old time by the will of man: but holy men of God spake as they were moved by the Holy Spirit."* In other words, *God* told these men the words to write down through their thought processes. Evangelist John F. MacArthur Jr. has stated that there are *four thousand passages in the Holy Scriptures that say they are the Word of God.*

Both the *Old and New Testament Scriptures* are entirely <u>true</u> because, first and foremost, there are various passages in these *ancient* writings that actually testify to their origin and to the *truthfulness* of that *origin*. For example, first of all, in the *Old Testament*, in the book of *Deuteronomy*, it says that *"He [God] is...a God of truth* and without sin, just and right is *He"* (*Deuteronomy* 32:4). A second verse appears in the book of *Psalms* (31:5) where the great *King David* of *Israel* proclaimed, "Into *your* hands I commit my spirit; redeem me, O *Lord*, the *God of truth*." A third passage appears in *Psalm* 119:151 saying, *"All thy commandments are truth."* In the fourth case (verse 160) in that same *Psalm*, the following is declared, *"Thy Word is true* from the beginning." In the fifth verse, *Psalm* 40:11, *King David* of Israel stated, "May *Your* love and *Your truth* always protect me."

New Testament sources are also prevalent. A passage proclaiming the *origin of truth* is the following: *"All Scripture is given by inspi-*

ration of God," taken from the book of *2 Timothy* (3:16). In other words, *God told all of these writers what to write (through their <u>thought</u> <u>processes</u>).* As an <u>eyewitness</u> *of Jesus, the great Apostle Paul testified of the* <u>truthfulness</u> *of God* when he said, in his letter to *Titus,* *"God, that can-not lie"* (*Titus* 1:2). The disciple *John, as another eyewitness,* reported that *Jesus,* in praying to *His Heavenly Father,* said, "Sanctify them [*His* disciples or followers] by the *truth:* <u>Your</u> <u>Word</u> is <u>Truth</u>" (*John* 17:17*). John* also heard *Jesus* say to *His* followers, "If ye continue in <u>*My*</u> <u>*Word*</u>, then are ye *My* disciples indeed; and ye shall know the <u>*Truth*</u>, and the *truth* shall make you free" (*John* 8:31–32).

Here's a hymn by Lynn <u>DeShazo</u>, titled *"Ancient Words."*

Holy Words long preserved for our walk in this world.
They resound with *God's own heart.*
Oh, let the *ancient words* impart.
Words of *life, words* of *hope,* give us *strength,* help us cope.
In this world where-e'er we roam,
Ancient words, ever *true,* changing me and changing you.
We have come with open hearts. Oh, let the *ancient words* impart.

Holy Words of our faith handed down to this age,
Came to us through sacrifice.
Oh, heed the faithful <u>*words*</u> <u>*of Christ,*</u>
Ancient words, ever *true,* changing me and changing you.
We have come with open hearts,
Oh, *let the ancient words impart.*
In this world wher-e'er we roam, *ancient words* will guide us home.
We have come with open hearts,
Oh, let the *ancient* **words** impart.

There is an additional, massive amount of evidence for the *truthfulness* of the *writings of the Holy Scriptures.* (the *Bible*). First of all, there are many *archaeological proofs.*

Peter Stoner, in his book *Science Speaks,* states that "many archae-ological expeditions have delved into the ruins of old cities referred to in *biblical accounts* and have *written reports* of their findings, show-ing that the *biblical accounts* were *accurate*." One such expedition was to try to find the *ancient* city of *Gaza*, a seaport on the Mediterranean Sea and one of five city-kingdoms of Philistia in the southern part of Palestine (spoken of in two books of the *Old Testament Scriptures: Zephaniah* and *Jeremiah*). Modern Gaza didn't fit the *biblical* descrip-tion. An archaeological search, however, did eventually uncover the *ancient* city. It was found buried under the sand dunes.

Since AD 1800, there have been numerous archaeological find-ings according to the excellent book, *"The Letter and the Scroll" that substantiate the accuracy of the Bible.* One of the most *ancient* of these was found in Sippar in southern Iraq. Several Babylonian clay tablets were found in the *ancient* library of the Assyrian king Ashurbanipal at the *ancient* city of Nineveh. They have been dated at 3000 BC and were inscribed with the story of a *worldwide flood* and called the *Epic of Gilgamesh.* There are many similarities to the *biblical* account of *Noah* and the *Great Flood* described in *Genesis.* For example, the epic tells of an original state of innocence of mankind, followed by temptation and sin, of a *great flood that covered the earth*, and an <u>ark</u> that was built in which only a man and his family were saved together with the seed of all living creatures. In addition, a British archaeolo-gist named Sir Leonard Woolley and his team excavated the city of *Ur* in today's Iraq near the Euphrates River. This had been a mighty city of the third millennium BC and the home of *Abraham* of the *Bible.* A uniform layer of clay eight feet deep was found that clearly had been deposited by *water.* Woolley concluded that it was "unmistakable evi-dence of a <u>*great flood*</u>—and one not less than <u>*twenty-five feet deep*</u>."

A granite boulder erected on Sehen, an island in the Nile River, was discovered by archaeologists. Called the *Famine Stela*, it describes a seven-year famine caused by the failure of the Nile to overflow its banks. This famine and the plagues that God sent to the Egyptians as punishment for not releasing the Israelites are all recorded in the *Old Testament*, specifically in the book of *Genesis* 41:54 and 45:6.

In 1933, in excavating the old city of *Dan* in northern Israel, a stone fragment known as the *Tel Dan Stela* was found. It is the *oldest nonbiblical text* that refers to the **kingdom of Israel and the**

House of David (King David's dynasty). It also describes other events just as recorded in the *Old Testament* **in both books of the** *Kings* **and** *11 Chronicles.* One description is of an encounter between *Hazael* and the p**rophet** *Elisha,* and another**, the war between the kingdom of Syria and that of Israel. The city of** *Dan* is described in the book of *Judges,* chapter 18, as having places of worship, court-yards, and an elaborate entrance gate complex.

In the *ancient* city of *Dothan,* there is a local tradition that a deep well found there is the very well into which *Joseph* was thrown by his brothers. (Genesis 37:17–24)

Recent excavations in the *port of Dor* confirmed the *biblical* account of the conquest of the Phoenician city by King David. (Ezekiel 27:4–5)

Archaeologists found written confirmation of the destruction of the Philistine city of *Ekron* **by the Babylonians in 603 BC. This disaster was recorded in the** *Old Testament* **in the book of** *Amos* **1:8.**

Ruins on a hill just to the north of Jerusalem is said to be the site of *ancient Gibeon.* The *Bible* mentions in *11 Samuel 2:13 the "pool of Gibeon"* as a meeting place of *Joab and the servants of David.* An American team of archaeologists uncovered the rim of such a *large pool* in *Gibeon,* and scholars think it may be the *same pool* as described in the *Bible.* It was thirty-six feet in diameter and eighty-two feet deep with a spiral staircase of seventy-nine steps leading to the bottom.

The earliest known *biblical inscription* was found in a tomb near Jerusalem and began with the words *"The Lord bless you and keep you."* These words date to shortly before the Babylonians conquered Jerusalem and were the same words recorded in the *Scriptures* in *Numbers* 6:24. This was a blessing that *God* had commanded *Moses* to confer on the people of Israel.

Archaeologists found at Samaria a *ring* which bore the *seal* of *"Ahab of Israel."* He was a very wicked king of Israel as recorded in *1 Kings* 16:30. They also found pottery with the name *"Baal."* In *1 Kings* 18:18, it is recorded that Samaria was a place where *Elijah* said that the people of Israel had "forsaken the commandments of the *Lord* and followed the *Baals.*"

In *11 Kings* 17:6, it is recorded that Sargon 11 of Assyria conquered Samaria and then Israel. This was *confirmed* by the discovery of a hexagonal clay tablet describing both events.

The prophet *Isaiah* **had predicted that Cyrus the Great of Persia would conquer the Babylonians. In 1879, the** *"Cyrus Cylinder"* was found in Babylon, which described that same event. (Isaiah 45 and beyond)

Now that I have demonstrated the various archaeological proofs of the *accuracy* of the *Old Testament*, it is time to state some of the archaeological discoveries that <u>prove</u> the *accuracy* of the *New Testament* as well. They are as follows:

In Israel, when excavating the ruins of the city of Caesarea in 1961, some Italian archaeologists found a limestone slab bearing the name of <u>*Pontius Pilate*</u>*, the Roman governor who* <u>*sentenced*</u> *<u>Jesus</u> to* **<u>death</u>** *by* <u>*crucifixion*</u>. (Matthew 27: 2–27)

In 2008, a polished stone called *"Gabriel's Revelation"* was found near the Dead Sea in Jordan. It is three feet tall and written in ink are some biblical phrases such as *"My Servant David,"* and *"Thus said the Lord of Hosts."* It also mentions *"a Suffering Messiah"* and *"a Triumphal Messiah."*

In 1968, a group of archaeologists found buried underneath a Byzantine church a house dating to the AD first century, which was later called *"The House of Peter."* It contained small fish hooks on the floor and a number of inscriptions that mentioned *Christ* and *Simon Peter.* (Matthew 4:18, 19, 20)

In 1956, excavations were conducted in eastern *Jerusalem*, which *uncovered a pool matching the New Testament's description of the pool of Bethesda.* This is the site where *Jesus* had healed a man who was unable to walk for thirty-eight years. (John 5:1–9)

In 1990, a tomb was uncovered two miles south of the old city of *Jerusalem*, which held an elaborately decorated ossuary containing the bones of a sixty-some-year-old man named *"Joseph Caiaphas."* The ossuary *was dated as being from the first century* CE, and the *inscription* was etched in the *Aramaic* language. The tomb may well be that of the *high priest* before whom *Jesus* was taken for trial. (Matthew 26:3–4)

In 1920, the University of Manchester, England, found on the *Egyptian market* the *oldest copy* in existence of the *Gospel of St. John.* This is a tiny papyrus fragment that had been in use in a provincial *Egyptian* town. This showed *how far Christianity had spread from Jerusalem* in Israel. The fragment was written in dark ink on both sides and contains verses from chapter 18 of John's Gospel. It *dates* to the *latter half of the first century* when *Jesus's* disciple *John, the fisherman Evangelist,* wrote this book as a <u>*very old*</u> man.

At Megiddo prison, part of a mosaic floor of an *ancient church* dating to the first half of the third century AD was uncovered in the late 1990s. It bore an *inscription* in *Greek,* which translated said, "*Donated* by Akaptos, lover of *God,* who contributed the *table to the god Jesus Christos* as a memorial." All of the above discoveries are listed in the book, "The Letter and the Scroll," published by The National Geographic Society

A fairly recent archaeological discovery **was of an** <u>*ancient church*</u> in Israel, in the valley of Megiddo. There was an *inscription* on the church that said, *"Jesus, the Son of God."*

Chapter 2

—*Luke* 24:44

There are many *prophetic proofs* of the *authenticity* of the *Holy Scriptures*.

The great author and theologian *Dr. D. James Kennedy* has stated in his book *Skeptics Answered* that "the *Bible* is *accurate* in its more than 1500 predictions *(prophecies)* concerning cities and countries."

Being a *prophet* of *God* in the *Old Testament* times was an extremely *serious* business. In *Deuteronomy* 18:22, *God Himself* said, "If what a *prophet* proclaims in the name of the *Lord* does not take place or come true, that is a message the *Lord* has not spoken." *He* also described what will happen to a <u>false</u> *prophet*. *God* declared, "A *prophet* who presumes to speak in *My* name anything *I* have not commanded him to say…must be put to <u>*death*</u>."

In his book *Science Speaks*, Peter Stoner has presented *scientific proof* of the *accuracy* of *prophecies* in the *Old Testament* relating to *Palestine* and many cities in the *Middle East*.

One prime example is a set of prophecies found in **Jeremiah** 24:9, **Jeremiah** 25:11, and **Jeremiah** 30:3. The first two describe how **God** is going to **disperse** the **Israelites** and the nations around them into all the kingdoms of the earth and have them serve the king of Babylon for seventy years. The third tells how **God** will cause the captive people of **Israel** and **Judah** to **return** to Israel and possess the land again. These **prophecies did indeed come true** when the

Babylonian empire took over Israel and the surrounding countries. The Israelites did come back later and established their nation in 1948.

A second example of a *prophecy* that was *perfectly fulfilled* is found in both *Isaiah* 13 and *Jeremiah* 51 regarding the future of the city of *Babylon.* Stoner says, "*Babylon* was one of the greatest cities, if not the greatest city of all times. Its walls were ninety feet thick and three hundred feet high. [This has also been *verified* by *Wikipedia*.] The rocks for the walls were imported at great cost. A river flowed through it, guaranteeing its water supply. There was enough land within its walls to supply it with food." It was very *self-sufficient*—not needing outside help to survive. A *prophecy* in the book of *Isaiah* in the *Old Testament* (written in 712 BC) states, "And *Babylon...shall never be inhabited,* neither shall it be dwelt in from generation to generation: neither shall the Arabian pitch tent there; neither shall the shepherds make their fold there. But wild beasts of the desert shall lie there; and their houses shall be full of doleful creatures." Similarly, a prophecy in *Jeremiah* concerning Babylon (written in 600 BC) declares, "And they shall not take of thee a stone for a corner, nor a stone for foundations; but thou shall be *desolate forever,* saith the *Lord.*" This *prophecy came true* after *Babylon* was conquered in 538 BC. The city, *to this day, is <u>uninhabited</u> by humans.* Jackals and many kinds of wild beasts live in the ruins, the rocks have never been moved, there are no sheepfolds there, and Arab guides will not even stay overnight there. The city is *truly desolate* just as the *Old Testament* predicted!

A third example is in another *set of prophecies* located in two separate parts of the *Old Testament,* namely *Zephaniah* 2 and *Jeremiah* 47. This set concerns the city of *Gaza* in Palestine. Both *Zephaniah* and *Jeremiah* predicted that *Gaza* would be *forsaken.* As stated earlier, an archaeologic search for the <u>old city of Gaza</u> was conducted, and it was found <u>buried under the sand Dunes.</u> I would say that's pretty forsaken!

A fourth example is in the book of *Amos,* in its first chapter. A *prediction* was made there that the *Philistines would perish.* They were a very powerful race of people, living in the southern part of

Palestine. There were *giants* among this race. *Goliath* was described in *1 Samuel* as being over nine feet tall. *Every Philistine has vanished as predicted!*

A fifth example is a *prophecy* about the country of *Egypt.* It is recorded in the book of *Ezekiel* 30:13 that "there shall *no longer be princes from the land of Egypt.*" History records that *during* the nearly *twenty-five hundred years* between this prophecy and Egypt's change to democracy, its *princes* were *never Egyptian.* They were from other nations who had conquered them, such as the Persians, Macedonians, Romans, Greeks, Arabs, Georgians, Turks, and Albanians. Peter Stoner says (concerning prophecies), *"These prophecies, and many more Old Testament prophecies all came true. We can then draw only one conclusion, and that is that God inspired the writing of every one of these prophecies."*

The *Tanakh (Old Testament)* is a group of *ancient sacred writings* that set forth *God's* definition of who the *Messiah,* the *Savior* from the punishment of the sins of humankind, would be. *Jesus* used the same organization of the *Tanakh* as is used today when He made the statement located at the beginning of the second chapter of this manuscript. He also said, *"Search the Scriptures…*they are they which *testify of Me"* (*John* 5:39), located in the *New Testament.*

According to the well-known theologian and evangelist Dr. D. James Kennedy, in his book *Skeptics Answered,* the *Old Testament writings (Scriptures)* contain over *333 predictions* of the *Messiah whom God would send to save people from the eternal punishment of their sins, provided they repented and trusted in Him for that salvation.* These predictions were made by many *prophets* who lived *hundreds* of years before the birth of *Jesus Christ.* Why so many prophecies? So that they wouldn't be missed! Using the *science of probability,* Peter Stoner in *Science Speaks* says that *"the chance that any man might have lived down to the present time and fulfilled just 8 of the 333 prophecies is 1 in 10 to the 17th power."* This number has 17 zeros in it. * *Yet Jesus Christ perfectly fulfilled God's definition of who the Messiah would be and is the* <u>*only*</u> *<u>one</u> who has perfectly fulfilled all 333 prophecies!* Peter Stoner, in that same book, has said that *he has provided numerical <u>evidence</u> that *this fulfillment <u>proved</u> Jesus Christ to be the Son of God,* the promised

*Savior. He even goes so far as to say that *"any man who rejects Jesus Christ as the Son of God is rejecting a fact proved perhaps more absolutely than any other fact in the world."*

A sampling of 29 of these *Old Testament messianic* prophecies and their fulfillment is as follows:

1. In *Genesis* 12:1–3, it is revealed that "the *Lord* had said unto Abram [later named Abraham by *God*], Get thee out of thy country…unto a land that I will show thee: And I will make of thee a great nation, and I will bless thee, and make thy name great; and thou shalt be a blessing… *and in thee shall all families of the earth be blessed."* That same promise was given to Jacob, another descendant of Abraham, in *Genesis* 28:13–14, where *God* said, "I am the *Lord God* of Abraham thy father, and the *God* of Isaac… *in thee and in thy seed shall all the families of the earth be blessed."*

   Fulfillment: *Jesus Himself* was a *Jew* and was also a descendant of Abraham_and Jacob and was truly a *blessing* **to all people. (All families of the earth include all Jewish families as well**.) The genealogy of *Jesus* appears in the *New Testament* scrolls in *Matthew* 1:1–2, 5–6, and this is how it is **stated:** "The book of the generation of *Jesus Christ*, the son of David, the son of *Abraham."*

2. *Isaiah's* prophecy in his book, in 11:1–2, 4, and 10, states, "And there shall come forth a rod out of the stem of *Jesse*, and a Branch shall grow out of his roots: and the spirit of the *Lord* **shall rest upon him…with righteousness shall he judge…in that day there shall be a root of** *Jesse*, **which shall stand for an ensign of the people: to it shall the** *Gentiles* **seek: and his rest shall be** *glorious*."
   Fulfillment: In mentioning the genealogy of *Jesus*, **the very beginning of the book of** *Matthew* **in the** *New Testament* **reveals that as** *Jesus* **was a descendant of Abraham (as stated previously),**

it follows that He was also a descendant of *Jesse* **(1:2, 5)** It states,
"Abraham begat Isaac...and Obed begat *Jesse*."

Lo, how a **Rose** e'er blooming
From tender stem hath sprung!
Of Jesse's lineage coming
As prophets long have sung,
It came, a flow'ret bright,
Amid the cold of winter,
When half spent was the night.

Isaiah 'twas foretold it,
The *Rose* I have in mind;
With Mary we behold it,
The virgin mother kind.
To show *God's* <u>love</u> aright,
She bore to us a *Savior*,
When half spent was the night.

This flow'r, whose fragrance tender
With sweetness fills the air,
Dispels with glorious splendor
The darkness ev'rywhere.
True man, yet very *God*,
From sin and death *He* <u>saves</u> us
And lightens ev'ry load.

O, *Savior*, child of Mary,
Who felt our human woe;
O, *Savior*, King of glory,
Who dost our weakness know:
Bring us at length we pray
To the bright courts of heaven,
And to the endless day.

3. Another prophecy relating to *Jesus's* ancestry is in the *Old Testament* in the book of *Jeremiah,* in 23:5. It reads as follows: "Behold the days come, saith the *Lord,* **that I will raise unto** *David* **a righteous Branch, and** a *King* [spiritual] shall reign and prosper, and shall execute judgment and justice in the earth." A similar verse is in *Isaiah* 22:22, which reads, "And the key of His father *David* will I lay upon His shoulder: so He shall open, and none shall shut; and He shall shut, and none shall open…and He shall be for a glorious throne to His Father's house."

Fulfillment: *Jesus* was a descendant of *King David.* **In the** *New Testament* **book of** *Matthew,* **the author's record of** *Jesus's* **genealogy includes,** *"Jesse* **begat** *David* **the** *King."* **This is reiterated in the second book of** *Timothy* **2:8, where it begins by saying, "Remember that** *Jesus Christ* of the seed of *David."* **A testimony to this same relationship of** *Jesus* **to** *King David* **appears in the** *Gospel* **(good news of salvation) of** *Luke,* **the first chapter, verses 68 and 69. It is stated as, "Blessed be the** *Lord God* **of Israel; for** *He* **hath visited and** *redeemed His* **people, and hath raised up an horn of** *salvation* **for us in the house of** *David."* **An additional verse in** *Luke* 1:32 **declares, "The** *Lord God* **shall give unto** *Him* **the throne of** *His* **father** *David…***and of** *His kingdom* **[spiritual kingdom]** *there shall be no end."* **This last verse occurs immediately after: "And thou shalt call** *His name Jesus.* *He* **shall be great, and shall be called the** *Son of the Highest."* **Lastly, in the twenty-second chapter of the book of** *Revelation, Jesus Himself* **speaks, "I,** *Jesus,* **have sent** *Mine angel to testify unto you these things* **in the churches.** *'I AM' the root* and the *offspring of David…"*

O Come, O Come *Emmanuel* (meaning God with us)
O come, Thou key of *David,* **come**
And open wide our heav'nly home
Make safe the way that leads on high
And close the path to misery

Rejoice, rejoice, *Emmanuel*
Shall come to thee, O Israel

In summary, according to prophecy, the *Messiah* was to be a descendant of *Abraham, Jesse,* and *King David. *Jesus perfectly fulfilled that requirement:* "Because the *Temple in Jerusalem* was *destroyed* in 70 AD by Titus and Vespasian, _all the genealogical records were also destroyed._ **Therefore, no one in the future claiming to be the Messiah could ever prove that he was the descendant of the above noted Jews"** (quotation from Dr. D. James Kennedy in his book *Skeptics Answered*).

4. In *Genesis* 3:15, it is reported that *God*, speaking to the devil (inside the serpent), said, "And I will put enmity between thee and the woman and between thy seed [descendant] and her seed; it shall bruise *thy head* and thou shalt bruise his heel." This means that someone from Eve's seed (descendant) will defeat the devil.

Fulfillment: According to the *New Testament*, as mentioned earlier, *Jesus* was from *Abraham's seed. He* had to have been from *Eve's seed* as well because *Abraham* was a descendant of *Adam* and *Eve. He* did hurt the devil's head (defeated the devil at his most vulnerable and crucial point) by *rising from the dead.* Therefore, in the end, *He* hurt the devil much more than the devil hurt *Him.*

5. **In *Isaiah* 7:14, it says, "Therefore the *Lord Himself shall give you a sign*; Behold, a** *virgin shall conceive, and bear a son,* **and shall call** *His name Emmanuel"* **(in Hebrew,** *meaning "God with us"*)**. * Emmanuel** is one of the many names for *Jesus* listed in the Holy Scriptures.

Fulfillment is in *Matthew* **1:18, 22, 23 and reads as follows: "Now the birth of** *Jesus Christ* **was on this wise… When as** *His* **mother Mary was espoused to Joseph, before they came together, she was** found with *child of the Holy Ghost."* Now all this was done *that it might be fulfilled, which was spoken of the *Lord* by the prophet *Isaiah* in 7:14, saying, "Behold, a *virgin* shall be with child, and shall bring forth a son, and they shall call his name *Emmanuel,"* which is interpreted as *"God with us." ******Emmanuel* **is one of the many names for** *Jesus* **listed in the** *Holy Scriptures.*

From heav'n above to earth I come
To bear good news to ev'ry home;
Glad tidings of great *Joy* I bring
Whereof I now will say and sing:

"To you this night is born a child
Of Mary, chosen *virgin* mild;
This little child of lowly birth
Shall be the *Joy* of all the earth.

Glory to *God* in highest heav'n,
Who unto us *His Son* has giv'n!
While angels sing with pious mirth
A *glad* new year to all the earth.

6. *Micah* 5:2 reveals a *prophecy* that says, "But thou *Bethlehem* Ephra-tah, though thou be little among the thousands of Judah, yet *out of thee shall <u>He</u> come forth unto Me* that is to be ruler in Israel; *whose goings forth have been from of old, from everlasting.*" (The *Son of God* would come in human form out of the little town of *Bethlehem*.)

Fulfillment: *Jesus* was born in *Bethlehem.* This is recorded in *Matthew* 2:3–6 as it states, "When Herod the king had heard these things, he was troubled, and all Jerusalem with him. And when he had gathered all the chief priests and scribes of the people together, he demanded of them where *Christ* should be born. And they said unto him, In *Bethlehem* of Judaea: *for thus it is written by the prophet, "And thou *Bethlehem*, in the land of Judah, art not the least among the princes of Judah: for out of thee shall come a Governor, that shall rule my people Israel."

Angels We Have Heard on High

Come to *Bethlehem* and see
Him whose birth the angels sing;
Come, adore on bended knee
Christ the *Lord*, the newborn *King*.

7. In *Isaiah* 60:6, it is stated that "they shall bring gold and incense; and they shall shew [show] forth the praises of the *Lord*."

Fulfillment: In *Matthew* 2:11, it is recorded that after *Jesus* was born, the Wise Men from the east in search of the *Christ* child, *Jesus*, "fell down, and worshipped **Him**: and when they had opened their treasures, they presented unto **Him** gifts: gold, and frankincense, and myrrh."

8. In *Hosea* 11:1, it says, "When Israel was a child, then I loved him, and *called my son out of Egypt*."

Fulfillment: When King Herod wanted to kill the baby *Jesus*, Mary and Joseph took *Jesus* to Egypt for protection against Herod. Later, after Herod had died, the family came *out of Egypt* and back to the land of Israel. This appears in *Matthew* 2:14–15. Here it is stated, "When he [Joseph] arose, he took the young child and *His* mother by night, and departed into Egypt: And was there until the death of Herod: *that it might be fulfilled which was spoken of the **Lord** by the prophet, saying, ***'Out of Egypt have I called my son.'***"

9. There is found in *Isaiah* 9:1–2 a prophecy which states, "Land of *Zebulun*, land of *Naphtali*...by the way of the sea, beyond Jordan, in Galilee of the nations—the people that walked in darkness have seen a great *light*, they that dwell in the land of the shadow of death, upon them hath the *light* shined."

In verses 6 and 7 of the same chapter, it goes on to promise, "For unto us a **child** is born, unto us a **son** is given: and the government shall be upon **His** shoulder: and **His** name shall be called **Wonderful**, **Counsellor**, the **Mighty God**, the **Everlasting Father**, the **_Prince of Peace_** [Sar Shalom]. Of the increase of **His** government and **peace** there shall be no end, upon the throne of **David**, and upon **His** kingdom, to order it, and to establish it with justice from henceforth even **_forever_**." (The **child would be God—His second personality**) (This will be explained later in the book)

Fulfillment: *Jesus* fulfilled these verses as recorded in the *New Testament* in *Matthew* 4:12–16. It reads as follows: "Now when *Jesus* had heard that John was cast into prison, *He* came and dwelt in Capernaum, which is upon the sea coast, in the borders of Zabulon [*Zebulun*] and Nephthalim [*Naphtali*]: *that it might be fulfilled which was spoken by *Esaias* [*Isaiah*] the prophet, saying, 'The land of *Zabulon*, and the land of *Nephthalim*, by way of the sea, beyond Jordan, Galilee of the nations; The people that walked in darkness saw great *light*; and to them which sat in the region and shadow of death *light* is sprung up.'" Note how *Isaiah* referred to *Jesus* as *"the Light."* This is extremely significant because *Jesus* had stated, *"I AM" the Light of the World: he that followeth Me* shall not walk in darkness, but shall have the *Light of Life"* (*John* 8:12).

Jesus also fulfilled verses 6 and 7 as listed above because He was born a *child*, had a wonderful <u>*miraculous*</u> *birth*, is the *Son of God*, is a <u>*spiritual*</u> *King governing His people* with <u>*unending perfect justice*</u> and <u>*peace*</u>, and was given all of the *divine* names that *Isaiah* listed in his ninth chapter. ***Jesus is [the second personality of] God, Himself!**

> 10. In ***Isaiah*** 35:5, the prophecy reads as follows: "Then the eyes of the blind shall be opened, and the ears of the deaf shall be unstopped. Then shall the lame man leap as an hart, and the tongue of the dumb sing."

****Jesus*** fulfilled this verse when during ***His*** three years of ministry on earth, ***He*** healed the sick as described in ***John*** 9:1–6 and 7 as follows: "As ***Jesus*** passed by, ***He*** saw a man who was blind from his birth. ***He*** spat on the ground, and made clay of the spittle, and ***He*** anointed the eyes of the blind man with the clay, and said unto him, 'Go wash in the pool of Siloam.' He went his way therefore, and washed, and came seeing."

St. ***Matthew*** describes in two different chapters of his book the healing works of ***Jesus***. In chapter 15, he records the following: "And great multitudes came unto ***Him***, having with them those that were lame, blind, dumb, maimed, and many others, and cast them down at ***Jesus'*** feet; and ***He healed them***." In chapter 11, ***Matthew*** records, "Now when John [the Baptist] heard in the prison the works of ***Christ***, he sent two of his disciples, and said unto ***Him***, 'Art ***thou He*** that should come, or do we look for another?' ***Jesus*** answered and said unto them, 'Go and show John again those things which ye do hear and see: the blind receive their sight, and the lame walk, the lepers are cleansed, and the deaf hear, the dead are raised up, and the poor have the gospel preached to them. And *blessed* is *he*, whosoever shall not be offended in ***Me***."

*At one point in *His* ministry, *Jesus* even proclaimed that *He* was fulfilling a prophecy from the prophet *Isaiah* **(Isaiah 61:1)**. This was reported in the *New Testament* by a prominent follower of *Jesus* named *Luke*, who wrote, "When *He* [namely *Jesus*] came to *Nazareth*, where *He* had been brought up, *He* went to the synagogue on the Sabbath Day, as was *His* custom. *He* stood up to read, and the scroll of the prophet *Isaiah* was given to *Him*. He unrolled the scroll and found the place where it was written: 'The *Spirit* of the *Lord* is upon *me*, because *he* has anointed *me* to bring good news to the poor. *He* has sent *me* to proclaim release to the captives and recovery of sight to the blind, to let the oppressed go free, to proclaim the year of the *Lord's* favor.'" And *He* rolled up the scroll, gave it back to the attendant, and sat down. The eyes of all in the synagogue were fixed on *Him*. Then *He* began to say to them, *** "***Today*** *this* **Scripture** *has been* **Fulfilled** *in your hearing!*" (found in *Luke* 4:16–21).

Hark the glad sound! The *Savior* comes,
The *Savior* promised long;
Let ev'ry heart prepare a throne
And ev'ry voice a song.

He comes the pris'ners to release,
In Satan's bondage held.
The gates of brass before *Him* burst,
The iron fetters yield.

He comes the broken heart to bind,
The bleeding soul to cure,
And with the treasures of *His* grace
To enrich the humble poor.

Our glad hosannas, *Prince of Peace*,
Thy welcome shall proclaim,
And heav''n's eternal arches ring
With **Thy** beloved name.

11. **Zechariah** 9:9 states, "Rejoice greatly, O daughter of **Zion**; shout, O daughter of **Jerusalem**: Behold, thy **King** cometh unto thee: *He* is just, and *having salvation*; lowly, and *riding upon an ass*, [donkey] and upon a **colt**, the foal of an ass."

*Fulfillment is located in the *New Testament* in *Luke* 19:28–31 and 35, where it states, "And when *He* (*Jesus*) had thus spoken, *He* went before, ascending up to *Jerusalem*. And… *He* sent two of *His* disciples, saying, 'Go ye into the village over against you: in the which at your entering ye shall find a *colt* tied…bring him hither. And if any man ask you, Why do ye loose him? Thus shall ye say unto him, because the *Lord* hath need of him"…and they brought him to *Jesus*: and they cast their garments upon the *colt*, and they set *Jesus* thereon." In the gospel of John 12:9, John relates saying, Much people that were come to the feast took branches of palm trees, went forth to meet *Him (Jesus)* and cried, *"Hosanna: Blessed is the King of the Jews that cometh in the name of the Lord."* *It is obvious that at first, the Jewish people honored *Jesus*.

12. In **Zechariah** 11:12, it is stated "If ye think good, give me my price; and if not, forbear. So they weighed for my price *thirty pieces of silver*." The betrayal by a **friend** was also predicted in another book of the **Old Testament**—in **Psalm** 41:9. The words are, "Yea, **mine own** familiar **friend**, in whom **I** trusted, which did eat of **my** bread, hath lifted up his heel against **me**."

*Fulfillment: Judas, one of the twelve original disciples of *Jesus*, betrayed *Jesus* for *"thirty pieces of silver,"*_as is recorded in the *New Testament* in *Matthew* 27:3–4 as follows: "Then Judas, which had betrayed *Him*, when he saw that *He (Jesus)* was condemned, repented himself, and brought again the *thirty pieces of silver* to the chief priests and elders, saying, I have sinned in that I have betrayed the innocent blood. And he cast down the *pieces of silver* in the temple."

13. Once again, in the Old Testament book of **Zechariah** 11:13, it goes on to say the following: "And the **Lord** said unto me, Cast it unto the potter: a goodly price that I was

prised at of them. And I took the **thirty pieces of silver**, and cast them to the **potter** in the house of the **Lord**."

Fulfillment: What happened to the *thirty pieces of silver* after Judas discarded them is shown in *Matthew* 27:6–9. We read there that "the chief priests took the *silver pieces*, and said, "It is not lawful for to put them into the treasury, because it is the price of blood". And they took council, and bought with them the *potter's field*, to bury strangers in. Wherefore that field was called 'the field of blood,' unto this day."

14. **Isaiah** 53:7 states, "**He** was afflicted, yet he opened not his mouth: he is brought as a lamb to the slaughter, and as a sheep before her shearers is dumb, so he openeth not his mouth."

Fulfillment: During *His* trial, **Jesus* did not try to defend *Himself* by trying to talk *His* way out of the accusations. This is all stated in *Matthew* 27:12–14 and also in *Mark* 14:60–61, and again in *Mark* 15:3–5. The excerpt from *Matthew* proceeds as follows: "And when *He* [*Jesus*] was accused of the chief priests and elders, *He answered nothing*. Then said Pilate unto *Him*, 'Hearest thou not how many things they witness against thee?' And *He* answered him to never a word; insomuch that the governor marvelled greatly." In *Mark* 14 (listed earlier in this paragraph), it is stated, "And the high priest stood up in the midst, and asked *Jesus*, saying, 'Answerest thou nothing? What is it which these witness against thee?' And the chief priests accused *Him* of many things: but *He* answered nothing. And

Pilate asked *Him* again, saying, 'Answerest thou nothing? Behold how many things they witness against thee.' But *Jesus* yet answered nothing; so that Pilate marvelled."

The Gospel Shows the *Father's* Grace

It sets the *Lamb* before our eyes,
Who made the *atoning sacrifice*,
And calls the souls with guilt oppressed
To come and find eternal rest.

It brings the *Savior's righteousness*
To robe our souls in royal dress;

From all our guilt it brings release
And gives the troubled conscience *peace.*

It bears to all the tidings *glad*
And bids their hearts no more be sad;
The weary, burdened souls it cheers
And banishes their guilty fears.

15. **Zechariah** 12:10 reveals that "they shall look upon *me whom* they have *pierced*, and they shall mourn for *him* as one mourneth for *his only son,* and shall be in bitterness for *him* as one that is in bitterness for his firstborn." And again in **Psalms** (the first book of the **Writings** from the **Tanakh**), in chapter 22, verse 16, it reports that "they *pierced* **my hands** and **my feet**." **Isaiah** 53:5 reveals, **"He was wounded for our transgressions (sins), He was bruised for our iniquities: the chastisement of our peace was upon Him; and with His stripes we are healed."**

Fulfillment: The **hands** and **feet** of **Jesus** were *pierced* as *He* was nailed to the tree for *His* forthcoming crucifixion. Later, *His side* was *pierced* in order to determine whether *He* had died. This is revealed, first of all, in the **New Testament** book of **John**, chapter 19, verse 34, which states, "But one of the soldiers with a spear *pierced His (Jesus's) side*, and forthwith came there out blood and water." **Verses 36 and 37 even tell that** *the prophecy is being fulfilled. These verses state, **"For these things were done, that the Scripture should be fulfilled... They shall look on him whom they *pierced.***" (from **Zechariah** 12:10). *In the action of *piercing Jesus's* side, the soldiers were able to prove that **Jesus** had truly died. This is very important to know, because there are those who doubt **His** resurrection, professing that **Jesus** didn't really die. Secondly, ***Jesus** fulfilled these prophecies in **John** 20:25–29 when **He** revealed to the unbelieving Thomas the *pierced* marks in **His hands** and **side**. It is written, "The other disciples therefore said unto him [Thomas], 'We have seen the **Lord**.' But he [Thomas] said unto them, 'Except I shall see in **His hands** the print of the nails, and put my finger into the print of the nails, and thrust my hand into **His side** [where the soldier had **pierced Jesus** in order to determine whether or not **He** had died], I will not believe.' And after eight days...saith **He** [**Jesus**] to Thomas, 'Reach hither thy finger, and behold **My hands**; and reach hither thy hand, and thrust it into **My side**: and be not faithless, but believing.' And Thomas answered and said unto **Him**, '(**Jesus**) My **Lord** and my **God**.' **Jesus** saith unto him, 'Thomas, because thou hast seen **Me**, thou hast believed: ****blessed** are they that have **not seen**, and yet have **believed**.'"

Christ, the **Life** of All the Living

Thou, ah! Thou, hast taken on Thee
Bonds and stripes, a cruel rod;
Pain and scorn were heaped upon Thee,
O Thou *sinless Son of God*!
Thus didst Thou my soul deliver
From the bonds of sin forever.
Thousand, thousand thanks shall be,
Dearest Jesus, unto Thee.

16. **Psalm** 22:7–8 reveals how "all they that see ***me*** laugh ***me*** to scorn: they shoot out the lip, they shake the head, saying,

'*He* trusted on the **Lord** that *he* would deliver *him*: let *him* deliver *him*, seeing *he* delighted in *him*.'"

Fulfillment: Both before and during *Jesus's* crucifixion, *He* was *mocked* and *insulted*. *This prophetical verse was fulfilled *during Jesus's crucifixion* as revealed in *Matthew* 27, verses 41 and 43. Here it says, "Likewise also the chief priests *mocking Him*, with the scribes and elders, said, "*He trusted in God; let Him deliver Him* now, if *He* will have *Him*: for *He* said, *I AM* the *Son of God*." More *mocking* took place in verses 39 and 40 of the same chapter in *Matthew*. Here it is stated, "And they that passed by reviled *Him*, wagging their heads, and saying, '*Thou* that destroyest the temple, and buildest it in three days, save *Thyself* [referring to a prior statement of *Jesus*, but one in which *Jesus* had meant the temple was *His body, thereby predicting His own death and resurrection*]. If *Thou* be the *Son* of *God*, come down from the cross." A third instance of *mocking* was seen in the book of *Luke* 23:36–37 where "the soldiers also *mocked Him*, coming to *Him*, and offering *Him* vinegar, and saying, 'If *Thou* be the *King* of the Jews, save Thyself.'" A fourth instance is in *Mark* 15:20 where it specifically says, "And when they had *mocked Him*, they took off the purple from *Him*, and put *His* own clothes on *Him*, and led *Him* out to crucify (nail hands and feet to a wooden tree and then suspend it upwards) *Him*." A fifth instance of *mocking* took place shortly before *Jesus* was crucified. This was revealed in *Matthew* 27:29 as follows: "And they bowed the knee before *Him*, and *mocked Him*, saying, 'Hail, King of the Jews!'"

17. In **Psalm** 22:18, it is next reported that "They part my garments among them, and **cast lots** upon **my** vesture [clothing]."

Fulfillment: While on the crucifixion tree, the soldiers **cast lots** for **Jesus's** garments. *This was fulfilled in *four* separate books of the *New Testament*. The *first* instance is in *Mark* 15:24 where it appears as, "And when they had crucified *Him*, they parted *His* garments, *casting lots* among them, what every man should take." The *second* account is in *Luke* 23:34, where it is stated, "Then said *Jesus*, '*Father* forgive them; for they know not what they do.' And they parted *His* raiment, and *cast lots.*" The *third* instance recorded is in *John* 19:23–24 where it is described as, "Then the soldiers, when they had crucified *Jesus*, took *His* garments, and made four parts, to each soldier a part; and also *His* coat: now the coat was without seam, woven from the top throughout. They said therefore among themselves, 'Let us not rend it, but *cast lots* for it, whose it shall be.'" The *fourth* account was recorded in *Matthew* 27:35 where it is revealed, "And they crucified *Him*, and parted *His* garments, *casting lots*: *that it might be fulfilled which was spoken by the prophet, 'They parted *my* garments among them, and upon *my* vesture did they *cast lots.*'"

18. ***Isaiah*** 53:12 states, "**He** hath poured out **his** soul unto death: and **he** was *numbered with the transgressors* [the sinners]; and **he <u>bare the sin of many</u>**, and made intercession for the transgressors."

Fulfillment: At *His* crucifixion, *Jesus* was *placed between two thieves (transgressors)* who were also being crucified. This fulfillment appears in *Mark* 15:27 and includes verse 28 as well. It says, "And <u>*with*</u> *Him they crucified two thieves* [who certainly would be classified as *transgressors*], the one on *His* right hand, and the other on *His* left. *And the *Scripture* was *fulfilled*, which saith, 'And *He* was *numbered with the transgressors.*'" It is reiterated in *Matthew* 27:38 as, "Then were there *two thieves* crucified *with Him*, one on the right hand, and another on the left." It is reiterated again in *Luke* 23:32–33 in which it says, "And there were also *two other malefactors, led with Him* to be put to death. And when they were come to the place, which is called *Calvary*, there they crucified *Him*, and the *malefactors*, one on the right hand, and the other on the left."

19. In **Isaiah** 50:6, it is revealed, "**I** gave **my back** to the **smiters**, and **my** cheeks to them that plucked off the hair: **I** hid not **my face** from **shame** and **spitting**."

Fulfillment: *Jesus* was *smitten* on the *back* (scourged) and *spat upon.* *This is fulfilled in *Matthew*, Chapter 27, verse 26, where it is revealed, "…and when he had <u>scourged</u> *Jesus*, he delivered *Him* to be crucified." *It is also fulfilled in *Mark*, Chapter 14, verse 65 as follows: "And some began to *spit* on *Him*, and *to cover His face*, and to *buffet Him*, and to say unto *Him*, *"Prophesy"*: and the servants did *strike Him* with the palms of their hands."

20. **Isaiah** reported in **53:3**, "**He** is **despised** and **rejected** of men, a man of **sorrows**, and acquainted with **grief**: and we hid as it were our faces from **him**; **he** was despised, and **we esteemed** [valued or appreciated] **him** not."

Fulfillment: ***Jesus was rejected by His own people*** (the Jewish race). In the gospel (meaning good news) of **John** 1:10–12, *this prophecy was made manifest as, "**He was in the world**, and the **world was <u>made</u> by Him**, and the world <u>***knew Him not***</u>. **He came unto His own**, and **<u>His own received Him not</u>. But as many as received Him, to them gave He power to become the sons of God, even to them that believe on His name**." Jesus was very saddened by the fact that *He* was rejected by *His* own race. In **Luke** 13:34, it is stated that *He* **said** the following: "**O Jerusalem, Jerusalem**… how often would **I** have gathered thy children together, as a hen doth gather her brood under her wings, and **<u>ye</u> <u>would</u> <u>not</u>**!"

21. **Psalm** 69:4 said, "**They that hate me without a cause** are more than the hairs of **mine** head."

Fulfillment: *Jesus was* certainly *hated without a cause*, because *He* did nothing wrong. In *John* 15:23–25, it is stated here by *Jesus*, "He that hateth *Me*, hateth *My Father* also. If *I* had not *done among them the works which none other man did*, they had not had sin: but now have they both seen and *hated* both *Me* and *My Father*." But this cometh to pass, *that the Word might be fulfilled that is written in their law, *"They hated me without a cause"* (Psalm 69).

22. This twenty-first prophecy revealed the ***purpose*** for ***Jesus's suffering***. *Isaiah* writes in his 53rd chapter, verse 5, "But ***he was wounded for our transgressions (sins)***, ***he*** was bruised for our iniquities (sins): the chastisement of our peace was upon ***him***; ***and with his stripes we are healed***." Verse 8 also reveals the purpose of ***Jesus's*** suffering as "***he*** was cut off out of the land of the living: for the transgression (sin) of ***my*** people was ***he*** <u>stricken</u>." Verse 11 continues to say, "by ***his*** knowledge shall ***my righteous servant <u>justify</u> <u>many</u>***; for ***he shall <u>bear</u> their iniquities (sins)***." In verse 12 of the same chapter, it says essentially the same thing, specifically, "because ***he*** hath poured out ***his*** soul unto death …and ***he bare the sin of many***, and made intercession for the transgressors (sinners)."

Fulfillment: *Jesus* was *stricken* and bore an *extremely painful death* in order *to justify us before God. By His blood sacrifice, He created for us a new relationship with our God because of the forgiveness of all of our sins (transgressions). This <u>loving</u> act of His assures us of our salvation, (ability to go to heaven after physical death) provided we believe that He did indeed do this for us, and we stay devoted to Him and His ways (trusting in Him).* *Fulfillment is found in *Hebrews* 9:28, in which is stated the following: "*So Christ was once offered to bear the sins of many; and unto them that look for *Him* shall *He* appear the second time without sin unto salvation.*"

23. In ***Psalm*** 69:21, it states, "They gave ***me*** also ***gall*** for ***my*** meat; and in ***my*** thirst they gave ***me vinegar*** to drink."

*Fulfillment: Shortly before *Jesus* was crucified, they gave *Him* vinegar to drink mingled with *gall*, and later, while *He* was hanging on the crucifixion tree, they took a sponge, filled it with *vinegar*, put it on a reed, and gave it to *Jesus* for *Him* to drink. This is recorded in the *New Testament* in *Matthew* 27:34 and also in *Matthew* 27:48 and again in *Luke* 23:36. *Matthew* 27:34 says, *"They gave *Him* vinegar to drink mingled with gall: and when *He* had tasted thereof, *He* would not drink." *Matthew* 27:48 recounts, "And straightway one of them ran, and took a sponge, and filled it with *vinegar*, and put it on a reed, and gave *Him* to drink." In *Luke* 23:36, it is revealed that, "And the soldiers also *mocked Him*, coming to *Him*, and offering *Him vinegar*."

24. Another prophecy in the book of **Psalms**, 22:17, states, "They **look** and **stare** upon me." It is reiterated in verse 13 of the same chapter as, "They gaped (a wide **stare**) upon me with their mouths, as a ravening and a roaring lion."

Fulfillment: *Jesus* was *stared upon* while on the crucifixion tree. This is recorded in *Matthew* 27:36, where it states, "And sitting down they (the soldiers) *watched Him* there." Verse 40 also mentions that, "there were also women *looking on* afar off."

25. In **Psalm** 34:20, it is stated, "**He** keepeth all his **bones**: **not one** of them **is broken**."

Fulfillment: The soldiers were instructed to break the bones of all those being crucified in order to hasten their death so that they could be buried before the Sabbath day arrived. This was a common practice in those days. Because *Jesus* was already dead, <u>none</u> *of His bones were broken.* The soldiers did, however, break the bones of the two thieves who were crucified next to *Jesus* (one thief on each side of *Him*). All this is reported in *John* 19. In verse 33 of that same chapter, it states, *"But when they came to *Jesus*, and saw that *He* was dead already, *they brake not His legs*."

26. **Isaiah** foretells in **his** book, 53:9, that, "He made his grave with the wicked and with the **rich** in **his** death; because

he had done no violence, neither was any deceit in *his* mouth." Verse 10 goes on to say, "Yet it pleased the **Lord** to bruise *him*; *he* hath put *him* to grief." Verse 11 continues, "*He* shall see of the travail of *his* soul, and shall be satisfied: by *his* knowledge shall *my righteous servant justify* many; for *he* shall bear their iniquities."

Fulfillment: After *His* death, *Jesus* was buried in a <u>*rich man's tomb*</u>. The verses in the *New Testament* referring to this matter are in *Mark* 15: 43, 45, and 46 and also in *Matthew* 27:57–61. The verses in *Mark* reveal, "Joseph of Arimathaea, an honourable counselor [a <u>*rich*</u> man], which also waited for the kingdom of *God*, came, and went in boldly unto Pilate, and craved the body of *Jesus*… And he gave the body to Joseph. And he bought fine linen, and took *Him* down [from the tree of crucifixion], and wrapped *Him* in the linen, and laid *Him* in a sepulchre which was hewn out of a rock, and rolled a stone unto the door of the sepulchre." In the verses noted in *Matthew* 27, it is stated even more clearly as, "When the even was come, there came a <u>*rich*</u> man of Arimathaea, named Joseph, who also himself was *Jesus's* disciple [follower). He went to Pilate, and begged the body of *Jesus*. Then Pilate commanded the body to be delivered. And when Joseph had taken the body, he wrapped it in a clean linen cloth, and laid it *in his own new tomb* which he had hewn out in the rock: and he *rolled a great stone* to the door of the sepulchre, and departed."

27. Three separate books of the **Old Testament** predict and promise that the **Lord** will be our **Shepherd**. King David, in one of his psalms, recognized this concept. In **Psalm** 23:1, he says that, "The **Lord** is my **shepherd**; I shall not want… *He* leadeth me beside the still [quiet and **peaceful**] waters" (so that I will have **peace** of mind). In **Isaiah** 40:11, **Isaiah** states, "*He* shall feed *his* flock like a **shepherd**: *he* shall gather the lambs with *his* arm, and carry them in *his* bosom, and shall gently lead those that are with young." Again, in **Isaiah** 53:6, it says, "All we like sheep have gone astray; we have turned every one to his own way;

and the **Lord** hath laid on **him** the iniquity (sins or wrong doing) of us all." In **Zechariah** 13:7, the words are the following: "Awake O sword, against **my shepherd**, and against the man that is **my fellow**, saith the **Lord of hosts**: *smite the shepherd*, and *the sheep shall be scattered*."

Fulfillment: In several places in the **New Testament**, this same concept is revealed. For example, in **John** 10:11, **Jesus** said, "'*I AM* the good shepherd: the **good shepherd giveth His life for the sheep**." In **Hebrews** 13:20, it says, "Now the **God of peace**, that brought again from the dead our **Lord Jesus**, that **great Shepherd** of the sheep, **through the blood of the Everlasting Covenant**." In **Matthew** 26:31, it is recorded that **Jesus** made a **prediction** to *His* disciples in stating, "All ye shall be offended because of *Me* this night: for it is written (in the **Old Testament**, in **Zechariah** 13:7], '*I will smite the shepherd, and the sheep of the flock shall be scattered*.'" *This prediction came to pass when *His* disciples <u>deserted</u> *Him* after *He* was arrested. In **1 Peter** 2:25, it is revealed, "For ye were as **sheep** going astray: but are now returned unto the **Shepherd** and **Bishop of your souls**."

Again, in **1 Peter** 5:4, **Peter** tells **Jesus's** followers, "When the **chief Shepherd** shall appear, ye shall receive a crown of glory that fadeth not away." **Jesus** also said, "*I AM* the *Door*: by *Me* if any man enter in, he shall be *saved*, and shall go in and out, and find *pasture*." This was recorded by one of **Jesus's** disciples, John, in **John** 10:9. In that very same chapter, verse 27, **John** also recorded that **Jesus** had said, "**My sheep** hear *My* voice, and *I* know them, and they follow *Me*: and *I give unto them <u>eternal life</u>*." **Sheep** have a tendency to **wander** off and run away from their *shepherd*. Those who wander away get into dangerous and uncomfortable situations and become frightened and anxious. They have not allowed their *shepherd* to take care of them or to lead them along the *__correct pathway__*. Therefore, they are *lost*. *God*, in *His* great wisdom, named *His Son* the *Good Shepherd*, using this illustration to show *us, the sheep, which "__way__" to go* in life so that we would have *__peace__* and *contentment in this life* and would eventually have *__perfectly complete__ "peace" and "joy"* in life eternal *in heaven* with our *Good Shepherd, Jesus*. As members of *His* flock, we need to *follow Him, praise Him, obey Him*, and *trust Him*.

Jesus is our *Shepherd*, well we know *His* voice!
How its gentlest whisper makes our heart *rejoice*
Even when *He* chideth, tender is its tone;
None but *He* shall guide us; we are *His* alone.

—H. Stowell

28. A prophecy in *Isaiah* 49:6 states, "I will also give *thee* for a *light* to the Gentiles, that *thou* mayest be *__my salvation__* unto the end of the earth." Yet another prophecy from the *Old Testament* book, *Malachi*, reveals in 4:2 that "unto you that fear *my* name shall the *Sun* [giving *light*] of *Righteousness* [*being without sin*] arise with *healing* in *his* wings; and ye shall go forth, and grow up as calves of the stall." Again, as stated previously, in 9:2, *Isaiah* predicts "the people that walked in darkness have seen a *great light*: they that dwell in the land of the shadow of death, upon them hath the *light* shined." In *Isaiah* 42:16, *Isaiah* mentions the same concept once more as he says, "*I* will make darkness *light* before them." In the first few verses of chapter 51, *Isaiah* gives hope to both the people of Israel and to the Gentiles as well as he bids them to listen to his words of the *light prophecy* as follows: "Listen to *me*, *my* people, and heed to *me*, *my* nation; for a teaching will go out from *me*, and *my justice* for a *light* to the peoples. *I* will bring near my deliverance swiftly, *__my salvation__* has gone out

and *my* arms will rule the peoples; the coastlands wait for *me*, and for *my* arm they hope…*my salvation will be forever,* and *my* deliverance will never be ended."

*Fulfillment is recorded in *John* 8:12, where *Jesus* said, "*I AM the Light of the World:* he that followeth *Me* shall not walk in darkness, but shall have the *Light of Life.*" *Jesus* is said to have also said, concerning *Himself,* "Yet a little while is the *light* with you. Walk while ye have the *light,* lest darkness come upon you: for he that walketh in darkness knoweth not whither he goeth. While ye have *light, believe in the light,* that ye may be the *children of light*" (*John* 12:35–36). *John* also mentions another statement of *Jesus* in 9:5, which reads as follows: "As long as '*I AM*' in the world, '*I AM*' the *Light of the World.*" This fulfillment is confirmed in *Luke* and also in *St. Paul the Apostle's second letter to the Corinthian congregation.* St. Luke recorded the role *John the Baptist* had in preparing the people for *the coming of Jesus Christ* when he wrote in 1:77 and 79 that John was to "give knowledge of *salvation* by the remission (forgiveness) of their sins…to give *light* to them that sit in darkness, and in the shadow of death, to guide our feet into the *Way of Peace.*" St. Paul confirmed the message of the *light* where he tells the Corinthian people, "For *God, who commanded the light to shine out of darkness,* hath shined in our hearts, to give the *light of the knowledge* of the *glory of God in the face of Jesus Christ.*" When *God* revealed to *Jesus's* disciple John *what heaven would be like, He* described it in the following words: "And the city had no need of the sun, neither of the moon, to shine in it:

for the glory of God did lighten it, and the *Lamb* [meaning *Jesus*] is the *light thereof* (*Revelation* 21:23).

I find it extremely interesting that Raymond A. Moody Jr., MD, in his book *Life After Life*, said that "*one of the common elements described to me by many people* who have been pronounced clinically dead and were subsequently *resuscitated back to life was** a spiritual encounter with a being of extremely brilliant "**light**."

The significance of *Jesus Christ's Light* is that <u>if</u> <u>we</u> <u>love</u>, <u>trust</u>, <u>and</u> <u>obey</u> <u>Him</u>, *it dispels the darkness of sin*, restoring us to a *new relationship with God*. It also *lights our <u>pathway</u>* as *He* leads us in the right direction throughout our entire earthly and heavenly lives. In this way, *we will receive <u>His best</u>*, and that will ultimately lead to our great "*joy*" and "*peace*" now and forever. In addition, it also *enlightens us to be reflections of His Light for all the world to see*. He says to each of us, "*Let your light so shine before men*, that they *may see your good works* and glorify your *Father* which is in heaven" (recorded in *Matthew* 5:16). St. Peter, one of *Jesus's* most avid followers, wrote that "ye should shew (show) forth the praises of *Him* who hath called you out of darkness into *His marvelous Light*" (*1 Peter* 2:9).

The radiant sun has vanished,
Its golden rays are banished
From dark'ning skies of night;

But **Christ**, the **Sun** of **gladness**,
Dispelling all our sadness,
Shines down on us in warmest **light**.

—Paul Gerhardt

29. King David, in *Psalm* 16:10, predicted the following: "Neither wilt *thou* suffer <u>*Thine Holy One*</u> to see <u>*corruption*</u>."

Fulfillment: *God's "Holy One," Jesus, was raised from the dead.* **His* body never saw *corruption*, just as King David had predicted. It was explained in detail by *Christ's* apostle Peter, in the *New Testament's*

Acts 2:29–32 as follows: "Fellow Israelites, I may say to you confidently of our ancestor, David, that he both died and was buried, and his tomb is with us to this day. Since he was a prophet, he knew that *God* had sworn with an oath to him that *He* would put one of his descendants on his throne. Foreseeing this, David spoke of the *resurrection* of the *Messiah*, saying, '*He* was not abandoned to Hades, nor did *his* flesh experience *corruption*' [as listed above]. *This Jesus God (the Father) raised up, and *of that all of us are witnesses.*"

Various accounts of *Jesus's resurrection from the dead* appear in the *New Testament Scriptures*. One account is recorded in *Matthew* 28. Mary Magdalene and the other Mary had gone to the grave site on the first day of the week and found that the grave was empty. *Matthew* relates that "an angel of the *Lord* descended from heaven, and came and rolled back the stone from the door, and sat upon it. And the angel said, 'Fear not ye: for I know that ye seek *Jesus*, which was crucified. *He* is not here: for *He* is risen as *He* said." The account of this same incident is recorded in *Mark* 16 and in *Luke* 24. An even more detailed account of this event, describing the actual **appearance of the Risen Lord to Mary*, is found in *John* 20. *Jesus* had actually spoken to her. John then said that following this event, "*Mary Magdalene came and <u>told</u> the <u>disciples</u> that <u>she</u> <u>had</u> <u>seen</u> the <u>Lord</u>, and that <u>He</u> <u>had</u> <u>spoken</u> <u>to</u> <u>her</u>.*"

John further relates, "Then the same day at evening, being the first day of the week, when the doors were shut where the disciples were assembled for fear of the Jews, came ***Jesus*** and stood in the midst, and said unto them, '**Peace** be unto you.'" In the same book, in chapter 21, John records, "After these things **Jesus shewed** [showed] *Himself* to the disciples at the sea of Tiberias… This is now the **third time** that *Jesus* shewed *Himself* to the disciples, after that **He was risen from the dead**."

Another account of Jesus's resurrection is found in **Luke** 24 as follows: It is related by Luke that two of them went that same day to a village called *Emmaus*…and while they communed together and reasoned, *Jesus Himself* drew near, and went with them…*and* **beginning at Moses and all the prophets, He** expounded unto them in all the *Scriptures* the things concerning *Himself*

…and as *He* sat at meat with them, *He* took bread, and blessed it, and brake, and gave to them and their eyes were opened, *and they knew Him!* And *He* vanished out of their sight. And they said one to another, 'Did not our heart burn within us, while *He* talked with us by the way, and while *He* opened to us the *Scriptures?* And they rose up the same hour, and returned to Jerusalem, and found the eleven [disciples] gathered together…saying, '*The Lord is risen indeed*, and hath appeared unto Simon' [Peter]. And they told what things were done in the way, and how *He* was known of them in breaking of bread." In summary, the ***Risen* Christ was witnessed by many people.

As a testimony, the apostle ***Paul***, in his first letter to the Corinthians, actually ***listed himself and many other witnesses of Jesus's Resurrection by name*** in his fifteenth chapter. He also stated that at one point ***after Christ's Resurrection, "Jesus was seen of above five hundred brethren at once."***

In the book *Skeptics Answered*, Dr. D. James Kennedy described ***the conversion to Christianity of Simon Greenleaf.*** "This man," Dr. Kennedy said, "is considered by many to be the **greatest expert on *evidence the world has ever known***." He was the Royal professor of Law at Harvard University during the end of the nineteenth century. He was challenged to investigate the authenticity of the resurrection of ***Jesus***, and after he undertook this task, he discovered that there was a ***tremendous amount of evidence*** and wrote a book about it. In *The Testimony of the Evangelists*, he wrote, "If the **evidence** for **Christ's resurrection** were presented to **any unbiased jury** in the world, they would have to **conclude** that *Jesus* of Nazareth **rose from the dead**."

The Resurrection of Jesus **proved** that **"Jesus is God"** (*His second personality*), the **only one** *who is "qualified" to save us from eternal torment.* **(if we believe, obey, and trust in Him)** Because *He* was resurrected, it means that we, too, will one day be resurrected. There are two references in the *Old Testament that describe the resurrection of the physical body*. The first one is in *Isaiah* 26:19, which states, "Thy dead men shall live, together with my dead body shall they arise. Awake and sing, ye that dwell in dust for …the earth shall cast out the dead." The second is located in *Daniel* 12:2. This verse relates, "And many of them that sleep in the dust of the earth shall awake, some to everlasting life, and some to everlasting contempt." *Jesus* Himself *reassured believers* when *He* stated, "'*I AM*' the *Resurrection*, and the *Life*: He that believeth in *Me*, though he were dead, yet shall he live!" (eternally) (*John* 11:25).

I Know That My Redeemer Lives

He lives triumphant from the grave;
He lives eternally to save;
He lives all-glorious in the sky;
He lives exalted there on high.

He lives, all glory to *His* name!
He lives, my *Jesus*, still the same;
Oh, the sweet *joy* this sentence gives:
I know that my *Redeemer* lives!

—Samuel Medley

Speaking of prophecies, a fairly recent finding, as reported in Michael Drognin's book entitled *the Bible Code*, is that of a *three-thousand-year-old prophetic code* in parts of the *Old Testament Scriptures*, particularly in the *Torah*, the first five books. "This code, *found only by computer, foretells*, in detail, many *events* which have already *happened fairly recently.*" I, as an author, wonder, *Could it be "the words... closed up and sealed till the time of the end"* revealed to Daniel the prophet *(Daniel 12:4, 9)*?

Are you of the opinion that Jesus Christ never existed? There is a massive amount of ancient, nonbiblical, historical evidence for the accuracy of the New Testament writings and for the life and teachings of Jesus Christ. The well-known theologian Dr. D. James Kennedy wrote in his book entitled *Solving Bible Mysteries* that "the *historical accuracy of the New Testament* has been *verified by archaeologists and historians.*" He cited the reports of *two great historians*. The first was Cornelius **Tacitus** (AD 55–120), who has been called the "greatest historian" of *ancient* Rome. He was an individual generally acknowledged among scholars for his *moral "integrity* and *essential goodness.*" In one of his major works, *The Annals*, he wrote that "*Christ* suffered the **extreme penalty** during the reign of Tiberius at the hands of one of our procurators, **Pontius Pilatus**." This is in complete agreement with the history of *Jesus's death* in the *New Testament*. Tacitus also made reference to early Christianity in each of his famous works.

The **second** great historian was a Jew named Flavius **Josephus**. In *Antiquities of the Jews*, he wrote about the census that Emperor Caesar Augustus had ordered to be done by Cyrenius, the Roman governor of Syria, for the purpose of taxation. This census was taken shortly before the birth of *Jesus* as recorded in the *New Testament* in *Luke* 2:1–2. *Jesus's* mother **Mary** and Joseph had to travel to *Bethlehem* for this census, and she was pregnant with *Jesus* at the time. In his writings, *Josephus* also spoke of *Pontius Pilate*, who sentenced *Jesus* to death by *crucifixion*. Later, he recorded, *******They reported that He [Jesus] had appeared to them three days after His crucifixion and that He was **alive**!*"

There were *other ancient historians* who recorded elements of *Jesus's* life, and these are all mentioned in the book "*The Historical Jesus*" by Gary R. Habermas. One *ancient scholar, Julius Africanus,* wrote that the *historian* **Thallus** had written about *Jesus's crucifixion* and the darkness and earthquake that covered the land during this event. This is consistent with the *New Testament* gospel writings. Another *Roman historian* was Gaius Suetonius **Tranquillas**, who was chief secretary of Emperor Hadrian and thus had access to the imperial records. He made reference to <u>*Christ*</u> and the <u>Christians</u> when he wrote about the punishment inflicted on the believers by both Emperor Claudius (AD 41–54) and Nero.

Habermas mentions <u>*many*</u> *other* <u>*ancient nonbiblical sources*</u> *for reliable historical information about Jesus.* Examples are *some ancient letters written by* **Pliny the Younger**, **Emperor Trajan**, *and* **Emperor Hadrian**. *Pliny the Younger* was a Roman author, administrator, and governor of Bithynia in Asia Minor. Bruce refers to him as *"one of the world's* <u>*great*</u> <u>*letter*</u> <u>*writers*</u>, whose letters have attained the status of <u>literary</u> <u>classics</u>." His tenth book of correspondence speaks about early Christianity in his province and also provides some facts about *Jesus*. He spoke of Jesus Christ worshiped as <u>*deity*</u> by early believers, the *singing of* <u>*hymns*</u>, and the <u>*teachings*</u> *of Jesus* regarding various sins. Pliny also mentioned his own method of dealing with believers, namely <u>*severe*</u> <u>*persecution*</u>. Emperor Trajan's reply to one of Pliny's letters also included his statement that Pliny was generally correct in his actions against the Christians, but with several restrictions. Another emperor who wrote <u>*letters referring to the*</u> <u>*trials for*</u> <u>*Christians*</u> was *Hadrian*, who explained that if Christians were found guilty after an examination, they should be judged and punished, but if the accusers were only slandering the believers, the accusers should be judged and punished.

An example of *another source* Habermas lists is the **Jewish Talmud**, which is a compilation of oral Jewish tradition from generation to generation. It <u>*tells of the death of Jesus on the eve of the Passover feast*</u>. A second one is a *written critique by* a second-century Greek satirist **Lucian**, which *supplies data about Jesus, His teachings,* and *His followers.* He mentioned that the *Christians believed they were* <u>*immortal*</u> and had *"sacred writings."* A third is an <u>*ancient*</u> <u>*letter*</u> *owned by the British Museum*, which was written by a Syrian named *MaraBar-Serapion*, who wrote to his son from prison, trying to motivate his son to emulate wise teachers of the past. It speaks of the <u>*execution of the wise King of the Jews.*</u>

There are other *second-century documents* deemed **Gnostic sources**, which provide *historical proof of Jesus and His teachings*. One such source called *"The **Gospel of Truth**,"* contains, among other things, that the *Son of God came in the flesh, that Jesus died, was nailed to a tree, that His death brought salvation to many, and that He was raised from the dead, putting on an eternal body*. **Do you still believe that Jesus never existed?

Another *proof* of the *existence* of *God* and the *truthfulness* of the *Holy Scriptures* is that *many only recently known scientific facts* were *revealed* to us *by God* in *the Old Testament (the Tanakh) thousands of years ago*. Many of these are illustrated in the booklet *101 Scientific Facts and Foreknowledge*. For example, the earth *was thought* to be *flat* for hundreds of years, but *God declared in the Old Testament* more than 2,600 years ago that the *earth* is a *circle (Isaiah* 40:22). The verse reads as follows: "*He* sits enthroned above the *circle* of the earth, and its people are like grasshoppers." *In medieval times*, the Bubonic plague killed thousands of people because there was *no quarantine* (isolation) for infectious disease, yet *God* had given the solution to that problem over 3,000 years ago when, as recorded in *Leviticus* 13:46; *He* commanded, "As long as he has the infection he remains unclean. He must *live alone*; he must live outside the camp (particularly significant in these days of the recent pandemic)." In the *Old Testament*, *God commanded* the Jews to *eat no pork (Leviticus* 11). Today, it is well-known that *eating pork* that is not thoroughly cooked *can lead to human trichomonas* (tapeworm). In that same chapter of *Leviticus* is a *warning against eating sea creatures that have no fins* or *scales*. We now know today that those creatures are *bottom-feeders*, which tend to consume waste and are *likely to carry disease*. *God* also *warned against eating* certain *animal fat*. *He* said, "Say to the Israelites: Do not eat any of the fat of *cattle, sheep,* or *goats*" *(Leviticus* 7:23). Today, it is an accepted scientific fact that animal fat is very dangerous to the coronary arteries of the heart and *can lead to heart disease* and *possible death*.

The theory of evolution would have us believe that over the years, the universe has become more and more complex. According to the booklet *101 Scientific Facts and Foreknowledge, evolution* is a *direct contradiction* of the known *scientific second law of thermodynamics* called entropy: This law states that everything in the universe is running down, deteriorating, constantly becoming less and less orderly. Modern science verifies that the universe is "growing old like a garment," just as it says in the *Bible* in the first chapter of the book of *Hebrews*.

"*Creation moments*" is a daily radio broadcast *presented by* "*Answers in Genesis*" about the **many extremely complex living things* in our universe. The program features *scientific evidences* of nature *that points* to **delicate design**, *not evolutionary chance*. Besides an infinite variety of plants and animals of this kind, the human body and its various organs constitute a prime example. On one of the broadcasts, it was revealed that "the *liver performs five hundred different tasks in the human body*. Structures like the liver have *caused many evolutionists to abandon the idea that life is a result of years of accidents*. The liver *is just too well-designed and integrated into the body to have been produced by purposelessness and mindlessness*."

God is not a liar! In the first few chapters of *Genesis*, the first book of the *Old Testament Scriptures*, it says, "In the *beginning God created* the *heavens* and the *earth*" and *"all the host of them."* He *completed this in just six days*. Evidence for this is located in *Genesis* 1, where on each day it records what has been created by *Him*,_and *after each day's creation*, the words, the *evening* and the *morning*, are clearly stated. Moreover, in *Exodus* 20:11, it has been clearly revealed that "*in six days the Lord made the heavens and the earth, the sea, and all that is in them.*" In the *New Testament's Mark* 10:6, *Jesus Himself revealed*, "From the beginning of the creation *God* made them male and female." The creation of both male and female is first listed in *Genesis* on the sixth day, the very same day that *our Maker* created the *animals*. Moreover, in the second chapter of *Genesis*, it is demonstrated exactly *how God* formed the animals and the man and the woman. Also, in verses 19 and 20, it says, "And out of the ground the *Lord God* formed every beast of the field, and every fowl of the air; and brought them unto *Adam* [the first man] to see what he would call them: and whatsoever Adam called every living creature, that was the name thereof."

This all means that there were not <u>millions</u> <u>of years</u> of evolution before the <u>first</u> <u>man</u> and <u>woman</u> appeared on the earth. There is <u>no real</u> <u>scientific</u> <u>evidence</u> (observable knowledge) for the theory of evolution, and it doesn't explain our conscience (which makes us feel guilty when we have broken *God's* laws) or any emotion such as *joy* either. The *Holy Bible* (*Romans* 2) mentions, "Which shew [show] the work of the *law written* on *their hearts*, their *consciences* also *bearing witness*."

The *Gospel* Shows the *Father's Grace*
Who sent *His Son to save* our race
Proclaims how *Jesus* lived and died
That *we* might thus *be justified.*

It brings the *Savior's righteousness*
To robe our souls in royal dress;
From all our guilt it brings release
And *<u>gives</u> the <u>troubled</u> <u>conscience</u>* "**peace**."

According to *Psalm* 32:9, *God* says, "Do not be like the <u>horse</u> or the mule, which have <u>no understanding</u>." Therefore, it can be safely concluded that *animals don't have* a *conscience. <u>We are not descended from an animal!</u>* The source of one of our emotions, *joy*, is plainly revealed by *God* in the *Old Testament* in *Psalm* 146. It states, "Blessed [made happy or *joyful*] is he whose help is the *God* of Jacob, whose hope is in the *Lord* his *God*, the *Maker* of *heaven* and *earth*, the *sea*, and *everything* in *them*." *Psalm* 4:7 says that "*God* fills my heart with *joy*," and in *Psalm* 16:11, it says that "You [*God*] will fill me with *joy* in your presence, with eternal pleasures at your right hand" (in heaven—the *Best Joy*).

In the book *Skeptics Answered*, Dr. D. James Kennedy proclaims that *God* has *revealed Himself* in *Creation*, in our *Conscience*, and in the *Light* of *Christ*.

According to **Romans** 1:20, "***since the creation of the world, <u>God's</u> invisible qualities—His <u>eternal</u> <u>power</u> and <u>divine</u> nature— have been <u>clearly</u> <u>seen</u>, being understood from <u>what</u> <u>has</u> <u>been</u> <u>made</u>, so that men are <u>without</u> <u>excuse</u>*" (to <u>acknowledge</u> <u>Him</u>). God** is longing for us to be drawn to **Him** in adoration because of **His** magnificent work. We are simply awed by the extreme *per-fection*, the *complexity*, the *intricate design*, the *orderliness* (such as the orbits in space), the *diversity*, and the *sublime beauty of* **His creation. In Psalm** 19, it is written that "the heavens declare the glory of **God**; the skies proclaim the work of **His** hands." All of nature is designed and is a true revelation of **His** majesty! *Who can see it and **not** believe that He really does exist?*

—Isaac Watts

All I have seen teaches me to trust the **Creator** for
all I have not seen. (Ralph Waldo Emerson)

Chapter 3

And *God made* the wild animals according to their
kinds, the livestock according to their kinds, and *all*
the creatures that move along the ground according to
their <u>kinds</u>. And *God* saw that it was good.

—***Genesis1***:25

**Biology text books today are filled with evolutionary ideas that
are presented as facts. The truth is that many famous scientists
believed in the existence of *God*, and they revered *Him* as the
Creator of all things.**

In *"Science Debunks Evolution,"* scientist Tom Phillips *lists*
many prominent scientists who believed in the Master Creator.
One such scientist was *Albert <u>Einstein</u>*, who has become an icon of
the twentieth century, his name synonymous with *genius!* He was
a world-famous physicist whose "relativity" paper (formulating the
link between energy and mass) formed the basis for the most famous
scientific equation ever written: E=MC squared. His work revolu-
tionized physics and made him world famous! He eventually won the
prestigious Nobel Prize in physics in 1921. Phillips said that *Einstein
stated*, **"The more I study science, the more *I believe* in **God**."

<u>Sir</u> <u>Fred Hoyle</u> was a famous British mathematician, physicist,
and astronomer. In London, *The Times* proclaimed: "Between 1945
and 1970, the range and significance of Fred Hoyle's contributions
to astrophysics and cosmology (the branch of metaphysics which
treats of the character of the universe as an <u>orderly</u> system) probably
surpassed those of any other scientist in the world." He was inter-
nationally acclaimed for his original work on stars, galaxies, gravity,

and the origin of atoms. He became the first director of the Institute of Astronomy at Cambridge University and had the distinction of being knighted in 1972. One of his main interests was in the *"origin of life."* Phillips cited *four declarations* of this famous scientist. The first is that "just as the brain of Shakespeare was necessary to produce the plays, so _prior_ _information_ _was_ _necessary_ to _produce_ a _living_ _cell_." The second is that "the Darwinian theory of _evolution_ is _shown_ to be *clearly* _wrong_." The third is that "_life_ cannot have had a random beginning…but *must have come from a cosmic intelligence*." The fourth is that **"the chance that life forms might have emerged in this way [speaking of evolution] is comparable with the chance that a tornado sweeping through a junk-yard might assemble a Boeing 747 from the materials therein."

Another quotation was from **_Ernst Chain_**, who won the **_Nobel Prize_** for Physiology and Medicine in 1945. His expertise was in the fields of biomedical research and biochemistry, the study of the chemical reactions in living animals, plants, and microorganisms. He was a key figure in making possible the widespread production and use of the antibiotic penicillin. In a speech made when he accepted a Doctorate of Philosophy Honoris Causa from Bar-Ilan University, Israel, Chain wrote, "We, the Jewish people, have had the extraordinary privilege to have been given a lasting code of ethical values in the **_divinely_** inspired [**_God-inspired_**] laws and traditions of Judaism which have become the basic pillars of the Western world." Chain's eldest son wrote, **_"There is no doubt that he (Ernst) did not believe in the theory of evolution by natural selection_**—he disliked theories in general, and more especially when they assumed the form of dogma. He also felt that **_evolution_** was **_not really_** a part of **_science_**, since it was, for the most part, **_not amenable to experimentation— and he was, and is, by no means alone in this view."_** **_Chain_** once said that, **_"To postulate that the development and survival of the fittest is entirely a consequence of chance mutations seems to me a hypothesis based on no evidence and irreconcilable with the facts."_**

Terry Mortenson creation scientist has done much research and has concluded that "the idea of the *earth* being *millions of years old* is the _greatest_ _myth_ ever forced upon the minds of men." St. Paul warns believers in *Colossians* 2:8, "See to it that no one takes you captive through hollow and deceptive philosophy, which depends on human tradition and the basic principles of this world rather than on *Christ.*" *Psalm* 40:4 also states that *a believer can lapse into believing falsehood.* It declares, "Blessed is the *man* who *makes* the *Lord his trust*, who does not look to the proud, to those who turn aside to false gods." *Mortenson* found that up until the late eighteenth and early nineteenth centuries, the *dominant view was that God created the universe in six days*, just as the *Bible* states in *Genesis*, the first book of the *Old Testament.* That is also *substantiated* in the second book of the *Old Testament*, namely, *Exodus*, in its chapter 20, verse 11. That verse clearly states, "In *six days* the *Lord made heaven* and *earth*, the *sea* and *all* that is *in them.*" Another verse in the *Old Testament*, in *Job* 12:7–10 tells it as it really is, namely, "But now ask the beasts, and they will teach you; and the birds of the air, and they will tell you; or speak to the earth, and it will teach you; and the fish of the sea will explain to you. Who among all these does not know that *the hand of the Lord has done this, in whose hand is the life of every living thing, and the breath of all mankind?*"

Old-age earth philosophical ideas didn't start with Darwin's book *The Origin of Species* published in 1859. In the early 1800s, various philosophers, naturalists, and geologists started writing books with their own various "theories." For example, one such philosopher was Comte de Buffon of France, who thought that the earth was seventy-eight thousand years old. In 1810, some came up with the "Gap Theory," which said that there was a great many years of earth's existence before human beings appeared on the earth. That theory can be easily refuted if you believe the **truth** of the *Bible*, which says in *Mark* 10:6 that "*at the beginning* of *creation, God made them male* and *female.*"

There is also much *evidence* of *dinosaurs* living at the *same time* as *humans*. There are various cave drawings of the two together, and dinosaur and dragon descriptions and pictures in Asia and Europe. Even in the *Bible*, in the book of *Job*, there is made mention of great beasts such as Behemoth and Leviathan. Numerous verses describing their fierceness and power are listed there. Verse 20 says that smoke goes out of Leviathan's nostrils and flame goes out of his mouth. Speaking of dinosaurs, **_T-rex bones have been found_** with _fresh tissue._

We have been told that it takes millions of years for muddy deposits to turn into rock. Science has now _confirmed_ what creationists who believe the _Bible_ have always suspected. There are _natural processes_ that _can form sedimentary rock within_ the limited time frame allowed by a literal reading of _Scriptural history (approximately ten thousand years)._ While digging some trenches in a salt marsh, a team of sedimentologists found stony nodules in the mud. Further research on how the nodules formed revealed that a mud deposit can be transformed into a layer of sedimentary rock in as little as _six months_! They found that _two bacteria are responsible for this._ One species gets its energy from the sulfates in sea water. In the process, it produces hydrogen sulfide. The second species of bacteria can do the same thing. But if there is too much hydrogen sulfide, it can also change iron compounds so that they react with hydrogen sulfide and other salts. The result is stony lumps of iron sulfide and iron carbonate-sedimentary rock that is _hardened quickly_ enough to _fossilize_ any animal before it decays.

The standard model for _metamorphic rock formation_ says that heat and pressure deep underground slowly force water out of certain minerals or crystals, changing or _metamorphing_ the rock. All the textbooks today say that it takes millions of years for such metamorphic rock to form. Now Yale geologists studying the process have discovered that under these conditions, _tiny droplets of water are expelled from the crystals much more rapidly than previously thought._ They have said that this _can happen in mere centuries_ or even decades. _This would easily allow for the origin of some of today's metamorphic rock to be traced back to the worldwide Flood of Noah on the timescale provided by the Bible_ (approximately _ten thousand years or less_).

****_There is so much order, complexity, and design in nature and in the complete universe_** (including the orbits of the planets and our own human bodies) **that it stands to reason that _there has to be a divine intelligent Designer_** (_God Himself_).

Scientist Tom Phillips also discusses _The Origin of Species,_ the book written in 1859 by **Charles Darwin**, the father of the theory of macroevolution (what evolution customarily means). Darwin was an **atheist** (one who did not believe in the existence of God) and, therefore, **didn't think there was a _Creator_ of all life** as we know it. **He claimed that life somehow arose from nonlife by chance, and then some forms of life "evolved"** into more complex forms through "mutations" (changes in the structure of genes) in cells. **Phillips points out the _errors_** inherent in this theory.

First of all, Phillips asserts "because **science** is based on **what we observe** in the physical world and logical inference from what we observe, _Evolution isn't even scientific. None_ of the _claims_ of Darwin _have ever been observed._ Man has _never_ been able to _create_ even a _primitive_ form of _life from nonlife._ Furthermore, _no mutations_ have _ever_ been seen to _cause_ a form of life to become a _superior form_ to the original form. On the contrary, **any mutations_**that occur **produce an_inferior** and **less-complex** form of that life. _Phillips_ also says, "An effective way to debunk evolution is to use Charles Darwin himself. The most _obvious objection against Darwin's theory_ is that of which Darwin himself conceded, and that is that _the world is not filled with infinitely numerous connecting links._ Also, the book _Evolution Exposed_ states that there is a _failure_ of the _fossil record_ to _display_ the _gradual nature_ of Darwinian _evolution._" We _always_ observe exactly what is _stated numerous times in the first chapter of Genesis: "Life reproduces_ 'according to _its kind_'"—i.e., cats beget cats, crickets beget crickets, etc. There are _variations in each of the_ "_kinds,_ but _they **never change into something else.**_"

Darwin has no fewer than _four chapters_ in _The Origin of Species_, which _present serious problems_ with his _own theory_! One such example is in "Chapter VI: Difficulties of the Theory," wherein Darwin touches on many things, including "design" questions in discussing _"organs of extreme perfection" (such as the eyes). Because he was baffled at the eye's extreme complexity_, Darwin is said to have told a botanist friend, "To this day, the _eye_ makes me _shudder._"

Darwin _did not have a scientific degree, and furthermore, he **assumed** that the **human cell** was "**simple.**"_ In those days, scientists did not have powerful microscopes to examine "cells." Tom Phillips also declares the following: "All life contains _DNA_, a genetic blueprint containing *information. Purely material processes cannot create infor-mation, which originates from a mind.* The DNA in **simple bacteria** has **several million** *specifications; man's has several billion.* Our DNA is unique because the odds of another person having our exact DNA are so remote we can dismiss that possibility altogether. *The DNA molecule, the most complex structure we know, and unquestionably the most efficient copying device, with self-correcting processes, prevents one life form from changing into another.* We are all copies of a copy, etc., going back to the very first human parents. By the way, the alleged 98 percent similarity of *human and chimpanzee DNA* is taught as proof of evolution, but the 2 percent difference actually translates into about *60 million base pair differences.*" In the *New Testament*, in *Acts* 17, *God* tells us that "*He hath made* of *one blood all* nations of *men* for to dwell on the face of the earth."

Of all religious books, **only** the *Bible has been proven to be histor-ically and scientifically completely true. According to the famous archae-ologist,* Nelson **Glueck**, "*Not one discovery has ever contradicted the Bible.*"

All things bright and beautiful,
All creatures great and small,
All things wise and wonderful,
The *Lord God made them all.*

He gave us eyes to see them,
And lips that we might tell,
How *great* is *God Almighty,*
Who has made all things well.

—Cecil Frances Alexander

Chapter 4

Jesus said, " *'I AM'* the *"Way"*…*no-one* comes to the
Father [goes to heaven] except through *Me*."

—*John* 14:6

Many people, especially in the twentieth and twenty-first centuries,
have experienced in this life *an added measure of "peace," "joy,"* love,
confidence, hope, and freedom from guilt, anxiety, and fear, by having a deep, loving, and trusting *conviction in their heart that Jesus* is
indeed the long-promised and long-awaited *Messiah* (*Savior from the
punishment* of *sin*) and the *Son of God.* They have been guided by *Jesus*
throughout their lives and have had a very loving, personal relationship with *Him.* This has happened because of *God's grace in giving them
saving faith* through hearing or reading *His powerful* **Holy Scriptures.**
In the *New Testament*, the eleventh chapter of *Hebrews* reveals that
"without faith it is impossible to please Him [God]: for he that cometh
to *God* must believe that *He is*, and that *He is a rewarder of them that
diligently seek Him." God tells us who His Son is in* the third chapter of
1 John, which states, "And this is *His commandment*, that we should
believe on the name of *His Son, Jesus Christ*, and *love one another."* In
the fifth chapter of *1 John, God reassures* each person who truly believes
and trusts in *Jesus* as his or her *Savior* when *He says*, "This is the record,
that *God hath given to us…he that hath* the *Son hath life (eternally in
heaven after earthly death)*; and *he that hath* not the Son of God hath not
life.* These things have I written unto you that believe on the name of
the *Son of God*; that ye may **know** that ye have *eternal life* [in *heaven*]."
Wouldn't you want to *know* how you will obtain a *happy* eternal life
after your earthly death? Wouldn't you *want to be* **sure** you have it?

No other religion or "pathway" to follow in this world will give you an assurance or guarantee of an entirely blissful eternal life after your physical death.

In the third chapter of *Exodus* (the second book of the *Old Testament*), when Moses asked *God* what *His name* was, *God* said unto Moses, "Thus shalt thou say unto the children of Israel, '*I AM*' hath sent me unto you." *It is extremely significant that when Jesus speaks of Himself, He tells us that He is indeed **God** (His second personality) by frequently starting with the words "I AM." For example, He said, "'I AM' from above… If ye believe not that 'I AM' He, ye shall die in your sins"* (*John* 8:23–24). *Sins* are those things that we think, say, or do that are *against God's Ten Commandments revealed in Deuteronomy* 5. *God* is without sin and our Supreme Judge. To die in your sins means that you will have *no forgiveness* of sins and will, therefore, *suffer* not only earthly death but eternal death as well (in the *everlasting torment* of "hell" where there is total isolation from *God* forever). The *Scriptures* clearly proclaim the *painful consequences* of sinful disobedience and lack of belief in *Jesus Christ*. For example, in *Romans* 6:23, it says, "The wages of sin is death" (physically and spiritually). A second verse reveals, "Be not deceived; *God* is not mocked: for whatsoever a man soweth, that shall he also reap. For he that soweth to his flesh shall of the flesh reap corruption; but he *that soweth to the Spirit shall of the Spirit reap life everlasting*" (*Galatians* 6). A third verse (*Proverbs* 16:25) indicates that "there is a way that seemeth right unto a man, but the end thereof are the ways of death." Another verse located in the second chapter of Paul's letter to the *Corinthians* explains this concept. It says, "The natural man receiveth not *the things of the Spirit of God*: for they are foolishness unto him: neither can he know them, because they *are spiritually discerned*" *(understood)*. St. Paul also wrote that "the god of this world *[the devil]* hath blinded the minds of them which believe not, lest the light* of the glorious gospel [good news] of **Christ**, *who is the* image *of* God, *should shine unto them*" (from his fourth chapter of his second letter to the Corinthian believers). "*Faith* cometh by hearing, and hearing by the Word of God" (Romans 10:17). In other words, *God works faith* *in Jesus Christ in a person's heart by hearing God's powerful Holy Scriptures. In His Holy Word, God clearly revealed Himself and the "Way" to eternal salvation (heaven)* when *He* said, *"God so loved the world,* that *He gave His only begotten Son, that whosoever believeth in Him (His Son, Jesus) should not perish, but should have everlasting life"* (*John* 3:16). *Jesus, God's Son,* said, "Go ye into all the world, and preach the gospel [the good news of salvation in *Jesus*] to every creature. He that believeth and is baptized [by the *Holy Spirit*] shall be saved: and he that believeth not shall be damned" (*Mark* 16:15–16). *He (Jesus)* also said, *"'I AM' the "Way," (to heaven) the "Truth," and the "Life." (everlasting)* **No one comes to the Father [goes to Heaven] except by Me**" (*John* 14:6).

O Jesus, King Most Wonderful!
O Conqueror renowned
O Source of "Peace" ineffable
In whom all *"Joys"* are found.

Chapter 5

My people are lost for want of knowledge.

—*Hosea* 4:6

Even in *ancient* times, the prophet Hosea was concerned about the spiritual depravity of his people Israel.

O come, *Thou Wisdom* from on high
Who ord'rest all things mightily
To us the <u>path</u> of knowledge show
And teach us in her ways to go
Rejoice, rejoice, *Emmanuel* (meaning *God with us*)
Shall come to thee, O, Israel

Reading the *Old Testament* gives a person vital knowledge regarding *God's promise* of a *Savior from* the *punishment* of *sin* (wrongdoing) and *His plan* for how *He* would accomplish that promise. Reading the *New Testament* gives one equally vital knowledge in how **God's plans* were *completely <u>fulfilled</u>* by <u>Jesus</u> <u>Christ</u>. In the *New Testament*, it is stated in the second epistle of *Jesus's* apostle Paul to *Timothy* that "the *Holy Scriptures…are able to make thee wise unto salvation through faith which is in Christ Jesus*" (3:15). According to the *Scriptures, people are not saved by trusting in their goodness and good works.* In his letter to the *Ephesians,* the apostle Paul clearly attests to this concept when he says, "By *grace* are ye saved, through *faith*; and that not of yourselves: it is the *gift of God: not of works,* lest any man should boast" (2:8–9). In *Romans* 10, it is again revealed by *God* that "they, not having knowledge of *God's* righteousness, and going about to establish their own righteousness, have not submitted themselves unto the righteousness of *God*. For *Christ [Jesus]* is the end of the law for righteousness to everyone that believeth." In other words, *God* will not look on us as righteous (holy) unless we confess our sins, repent of them (turn away from them), ask *Jesus* for forgiveness, and have faith and trust in *Jesus, God's Son, who kept the law for us and suffered the punishment that we deserve as sinners*—as people who cannot possibly completely obey *God's* laws no matter how much we try. *God* told us in the *Old Testament*, in *Ecclesiastes* 7:20, that *"there is not a just man upon the earth, that doeth good, and sinneth not,"* and *Isaiah* 64:6 that "all of our righteousnesses are as filthy rags" in *God's* sight. *He* has also said in Romans 3, *"Therefore by the deeds of the law there shall no flesh be justified in His sight: for by the law is the knowledge of sin."* However, fortunately, *God* has also revealed to us in *Romans* 4 that *"to him that…believeth on Him (Jesus) that justifieth the ungodly, his faith is counted for righteousness, (being morally right)"* and in chapter 5, that *"therefore being justified by faith, we have "peace" with God through our Lord Jesus Christ* …being now justified by *His* blood, *we shall be saved from wrath through Him,"* and in chapter 10, that "if thou shalt confess with thy mouth the *Lord Jesus*, and shalt believe in thine heart that *God* raised *Him* from the dead, thou shalt be saved." **Only* through *His Holy Word*, the *Holy *Scriptures, has God given* and continues to give individuals *saving faith*. That faith *dispels* all *fear* of *death* and, therefore, gives us that tremendous feeling of *"peace"* and *"joy"* that we all crave.

For by **grace** are ye saved, through **faith**; and that not of your-selves: It is the *gift* of *God: Not* of *works*, lest any man should boast. (*Ephesians* 2:8–9)

Chapter 6

Let *us* make man in *our* image, after *our* likeness.

—(The *Holy Trinity*, Genesis 1:26)

Recently, many Jewish people, as well as Gentiles, have received saving faith in *Jesus*. The Jewish believers are called messianic Jews, and they worship together in Jewish messianic congregations throughout America and abroad. *They have retained their Jewish heritage and traditions while at the same time believing and trusting in Jesus for <u>forgiveness</u> and for their <u>eternal</u> <u>salvation</u>.* These Jewish people have come to understand what influenced and flawed the thinking of many of the Jews at the time of *Jesus's* ministry. The Jews at that point in time were influenced by the revolt of the Maccabean Jews against the merciless tyranny and religious intolerance of Syria, which had occurred in approximately 167 BC. This is recorded in the *History Resource Article* called "*The Revolt of the Maccabees*." It reads as follows: "Thousands of Jews had been killed for their religious beliefs. Because the Maccabees had stood up for their beliefs, they were highly honored and revered as liberating military heroes. Years later, when *Rome* took over the Jewish government, the Jews *eagerly awaited* and anticipated *another <u>great</u> <u>military</u> Messiah [Savior] instead of a <u>spiritual</u> Messiah*—someone who would become *King* and offer them salvation from the humiliating bondage and tyranny of *Rome*. The Jewish concept of the *Messiah* had become <u>warped</u> and *twisted.*"

They, thus, *completely rejected Jesus's offer* of becoming their <u>spiritual</u> *King—one who offered them salvation* from *God's punishment* of *their sins (forgiveness)* and *eternal salvation* of their *souls. He still reaches out to them today.*

According to the well-known theologian Dr. D. James Kennedy, in his book *Solving Bible Mysteries*, there was a *former rabbi*, named *Leopold Cohn* (who later became a messianic Jew—one who believes in *Jesus* as the *Messiah*), who *discovered that the Jews had also been led astray by their greatest theologian, Moses Maimonides*. Maimonides was the one who compiled the Jewish Creed. *The Jews rejected the concept of God as having several personalities (Father, Son,* and *Holy Spirit)* and yet remaining *one God* because *Maimonides substituted the Hebrew word yachid* for the original Hebrew word *achad when speaking of the oneness of God.*

Achad means "one unity of essence but a diversity of personalities." Achad was the exact word that *God* selected when *He* inspired *Moses* to write the *Shema* in the *Old Testament* book of *Deuteronomy*, in 6:4 ("Hear, O Israel: The *Lord* our *God* is one *Lord*"). In using the Hebrew word *achad, God* was telling us that *He* is a unity of essence but *has several personalities*. In addition, Hebrew scholars say that there are *three numbers in the Hebrew language*. The word for singular means one, the word for dual means two, and *the word* for *plural means more than two.* The *Hebrew word for God* in *Genesis* 1:1, the first book of the *Old Testament Scriptures*, is *Elohim*, which is *plural*. Therefore, God is only *one God but* is *made up of more than two personalities.*

There are many times in the *Old Testament* where *God* is referred to in the *plural* form. For example, in *Genesis* 1:26, *God speaks in plural* when *He says*, "Let *us* make man in *our* image, after *our* likeness." In *Genesis* 3:22, *God speaks*, saying, "Behold, the man is become as one of *us*, to know good and evil." Again, in *Genesis* 11:7 *God says*, "Go to, let *us* go down [to the Tower of Babel] and there confound their language." In addition, in *Isaiah* 6:8, when *Isaiah heard* the voice of the *Lord saying*, "Whom shall I send, and who will go for *us*?" He answered, "Here am I, send me!" This *three-person unity of God* may be more easily understood if one thinks of it in terms of the *analogy* of *a three-sided pretzel.* Each part has an identity and personality of its own, yet *all three* parts are *one.*

Dr. Kennedy further stated in his book that in *Genesis* 49:10, it was *predicted* that "*the scepter shall not depart from Judah*, nor a lawgiver from between his feet, *until Shiloh comes*." He said that ***Shiloh is another name for the Messiah*, so that *this prophecy not only predicts the coming of the Messiah but states* that the *Messiah must come before* the *scepter* (the right to execute a person for a crime) was *taken away* (Genesis 49:10) from the *Jews* by the Roman government a little more than forty years before the destruction of the *Temple*. This fact is located in the *Palestinian Talmud*, an ancient collection of Jewish civil and religious law. It is also listed in *Antiquities of the Jews* (20:9), written by *Josephus*, a noted Jewish general and *historian*. Dr. Kennedy pronounced that *while the Jewish leaders in Jerusalem wept and bemoaned the loss of the scepter, a boy of about twelve years old was growing up in Nazareth*, *the living fulfillment of God's promise. This was *Jesus* of Nazareth, *Shiloh*, the *long-awaited Messiah. He had come before the scepter was removed, as promised.* *According to prophecy, it is <u>impossible</u> for the Messiah to come in the future. **He has to have already come!**

According to the *Old Testament*, the *Messiah was to be a descendant of Abraham, Jacob, and King David.* In 70 AD, the second Temple was completely destroyed by the Roman army under Titus and Vespasian. Therefore, *all* the *genealogical records* that were *stored* in the *Temple* were also *destroyed.* <u>How could anyone</u> in <u>the future claiming</u> to <u>be</u> *the Messiah* <u>ever</u> be <u>able</u> to <u>prove it</u>?

There are <u>many other reasons why</u> the Jewish people should <u>accept</u> Jesus as their Messiah. One is that *Jesus was*, in fact, *Jewish*! Michael L. Brown, in his book *Answering Jewish Objections to Jesus*, made some very pertinent statements. He said that *"Jesus is <u>the most influential Jew</u> ever to walk the earth"* (page 22) that *"the *Torah [the first five books of the Old Testament] along with the rest of the Hebrew Scriptures points to Jesus the Messiah"* (page 18), and that "at first His Jewish followers thought that *Jesus* came to save the Jews only! (page 16). Brown also brought out the fact that "*according to* B. Yoma 39b of the *Jewish Talmud, God did not accept the sacrifices* that were offered on the Day of Atonement for the last forty years before the destruction of the Second Temple <u>[from 30 to 70 CE]</u>. What **great event** happened *in the year 30?* **Jesus** was <u>**rejected**</u> by **His** own people and crucified. ***God no longer accepted** the atonement <u>**sacrifices because He was satisfied that** **His Son, Jesus, the Messiah,**</u> had just <u>**offered Himself**</u> as the <u>***perfect final sacrifice***</u>!" (page 74).

According to the *Old Testament* (Tanakh), *God had a plan to give His chosen people, the Jewish people, the chance to be saved* before the end of the world. *He originally closed their eyes to the <u>truth</u>* as explained in *Isaiah* 29:10. There it states, "For the *Lord* hath poured out upon you the spirit of deep sleep, and hath closed your eyes." St. Paul pointed out in the entire *Romans* 11, namely, "*According* as it is written, God hath given them the spirit of slumber, eyes that they should not see, and ears that they should not hear unto this day. And David saith, Let their table be made a snare, and a trap, and a stumblingblock, and a recompence unto them: Let their eyes be darkened, that they may not see, and bow down their back always. I say then, Have they stumbled that they shall fall? *God* forbid: but rather through their fall, salvation is come unto the Gentiles, for to provoke them to jealousy."

There is still *hope* for *salvation* for the *Jewish people if they believe* and *trust* in *Jesus* as their *Messiah* as stated in verses 23 and 25 of the book of Romans 11, "And they also, if they abide not still in unbelief, shall be graffed in: for *God is able to graff them in again*," and "blindness in part is happened to Israel, until the fullness of the Gentiles be come in."

***Today there are tens of thousands of Jews who truly believe in Jesus as their Messiah (called Messianic Jews).*

Many of them are highly educated, and some are even ordained rabbis. *They have <u>not</u> lost their Jewish heritage.* They have gained *"joy"*, and *freedom from the fear of death.* Trusting in *Jesus's* brutal *sacrificial death for them* has cast out that fear. *These Messianic Jews* choose to worship together in any of the *many **Jewish messianic synagogues*** or congregations *available. These* **synagogues retain the Jewish traditions and celebrate all the Jewish holidays**, but also **trust in Jesus as the promised Messiah.** Messianic Jews wish to be with other Jews who share their conviction, and they are not ashamed of believing and trusting in *Jesus* as their *Messiah. Jesus Himself* warned of the consequences of being ashamed of *Him. He plainly said, "Whoever, therefore, shall be ashamed of Me, and of My Words…of him also shall the Son of Man be ashamed, when He cometh in the glory of His Father with the holy angels"* (Mark 8:38).

<u>*Sadly,*</u> *many generations of Jewish people have continued to <u>reject</u> Jesus as their spiritual Messiah. (Savior)* In many cases, the Jews have been instructed to never read anything that might cause them to change their mind. They have completely obeyed those commands. I also recently heard that *in many cases, **the book of <u>**Isaiah**</u> (in the Old Testament) has been <u>withheld from them</u>*. These people, therefore, have not read ***chapter 53** of that book, which contains *numerous prophecies* (predictions) *about Jesus Christ*, made by the prophet Isaiah—*prophecies *that all came true* in the person of <u>*Jesus Christ*</u>. **Another important book* also has *many prophecies*, all of which were *completely fulfilled by Jesus*. These prophecies *are* in **chapter 22** of the book of **Psalms**. It is *vitally important* to personally *read* these *books*, thereby *examining the evidence*. If you are a Jewish person, I strongly urge you to read what *God* is trying to convey to you. During *His* three years of public ministry, *Jesus tried many times to reach out in love to people of His own race*. When speaking of them, *He said, *"How often have I* desired to gather your children together as a hen gathers her brood under her wings, but <u>*you would not*</u>" (*Luke* 13:34). *He* still reaches out to you today. <u>*Won't you give Him a chance to enter your heart so that you can be saved from a fearful and less joyous earthly life and a truly miserable eternal life after death?*</u>

Chapter 7

Holy, Holy, Holy,
Lord God Almighty!
All *Thy* works shall praise *Thy* name
In earth and sky and sea;

Holy, Holy, Holy!
Merciful and Mighty
God in *Three Persons,*
Blessed Trinity!

—Reginald Heber

For there are *three* that bear record in heaven, the *Father*, the *Word* [*God's Son, Jesus*], and the *Holy Ghost*: and these <u>*three*</u> are <u>*one*</u>.

—*1 John 5:7*

The First Personality

The *first* personality of *God* is the *Heavenly Father. God* is referred to in this way in the *Old Testament* in *Isaiah* 64:8, which states, "But now, O *Lord*, thou art our *Father*; we are the clay, and *thou* our potter; and we all are the work of *thy* hand." Again in *Psalm* 68:5, it is revealed that

"a father of the fatherless…is *God* in his holy habitation." *Jesus* constantly referred to *His Father* in heaven. In the garden of Gethsemane, shortly before *His* crucifixion, *He* prayed, "O *My Father*, if it be possible, let this cup pass from *Me*: Nevertheless not as *I* will, but as *Thou* wilt" (*Matthew* 26:39). The most well-known mention of *God* the *Father* was when *Jesus* taught the multitudes The *Lord's Prayer*, which begins, "Our *Father which* art in heaven..." (*Matthew* 6:9).

The Second Personality

God, however, has *two more personalities*. The *second* personality of *God* is the *Son of God. He is mentioned numerous times in the New Testament.* In fact, the *New Testament* contains the complete history of *God's Son's* life on this very earth. Several particularly significant instances in which *God's Son* is mentioned are as follows: In two separate events of *Jesus's* life, *His Heavenly Father*, testified that *Jesus* was *His Son*. The first event occurred during *Jesus's* baptism by *John the Baptist*. St. *Matthew*, as an eyewitness, related this scene in his third chapter, verses 16 and 17 as he stated the following: "*Jesus*, when *He* was baptized, went up straightway out of the water: and lo, the heavens were opened unto *Him*, and *He* saw the *Spirit of God* descending like a dove, and lighting upon *Him*: and lo a *voice* from heaven, saying, '*This* is *My beloved Son, in whom "I AM" well pleased.*"

In the second event, *Jesus's transfiguration (His appearance in radiant glory)* occurred on a high mountain and was witnessed by Peter, James, and John. They saw that "*His* face did shine as the sun, and *His* raiment was white as the light." *Jesus* again heard *His Heavenly Father's voice*. This is related to us in the following words:

"While he [Peter] yet spake, Behold, a bright cloud overshadowed them: and behold a *voice out of the cloud, which said, 'This* is *My beloved Son*, in whom "*I AM*" well pleased. Hear ye *Him*" *(Matthew* 17:5).

There were <u>*other eyewitnesses*</u> who recorded instances where *Jesus* was proclaimed to be *God's Son*.

John, one of *Jesus's* faithful followers, in the first chapter of his book, stated that after seeing *Jesus, John the Baptist* proclaimed, "I saw, and bare record that this is the *Son of God*." And in the first letter of *John*, 4:9, John states, "In this was manifested the *love of God toward us*, because that *God* sent *His only begotten Son* into the world, *that we might live [eternally] through Him*."

When one of the centurions, and they that were with Him [during the crucifixion] saw the earthquake and those things that were done, they feared greatly saying, "Truly this was the *Son of God*." (Matthew 27:54 KJV)

The *Son of God* is mentioned in several *Old Testament* books as well. First of all, in *Psalm* 2:7, it is related, "*I* will declare the decree: the *Lord* hath said unto **Me**, *Thou art My Son; this day have I begotten Thee*." Verification that **Jesus fulfilled this verse is located in the New Testament*, in *Acts* (of the Apostles) 13:32–33 where it states, "And we declare unto you glad tidings, how that *the *promise* which was made unto the fathers, *God hath fulfilled the same* unto us their children, in that *He* hath raised up *Jesus* again; *as it is also written in the second psalm (from the Old Testament), Thou art My Son, this day have I begotten Thee*." Again in verses 11 and 12 of the same *Psalm*, it says, "Serve the *Lord* with fear, and rejoice with trembling. Do homage in purity [the Hebrew word used here is *bar* which, according to the Jewish Study Bible (page 1286) can also mean "*son*," especially in Aramaic, and this has sometimes been connected to the *divinely adopted son* mentioned (above) in verse seven of *Psalm* 2) lest *He* [the *Son*] be angry, and ye perish from the way, when *His* wrath is kindled but a little. *Blessed are all they that put their trust in Him*."

Second of all, *Isaiah*, a major *Old Testament prophet, also mentioned the Son* in his prophetic book. He predicted, "For unto us a *child* is born, unto us a *son* is given: and the government shall be upon *his* shoulder [*He* will be a *King*-spiritually]: and *His name* shall be called *Wonderful* [in Hebrew, meaning *miraculous*], *Counsellor* (full of wisdom), the *Mighty God*, the *Everlasting Father*, the *Prince of Peace*. Of the increase of *His* government and *"peace"* there shall be no end, upon the throne of David, and upon *His* kingdom, to order it, and to establish it with <u>judgment</u> and with <u>justice</u> from henceforth *even <u>forever</u>*. The zeal of the *Lord of Hosts* will perform this" (*Isaiah* 9:6–7). In other words, *a child will be born who is God's Son, the second of the three personalities of God Himself. Only God could have a spiritual kingdom* that *would last <u>forever</u>*. Again, in chapter 7 of the very same book, *Isaiah also predicted*, "Therefore *the Lord Himself shall give you a <u>sign</u>*; Behold, *a virgin shall conceive, and bear a son, and shall call his name Immanuel* [which means *God with us*]." **Fulfillment* of this prophecy is found *in the New Testament* in *Luke* 1:30–35. As you will see, *many of the words are strikingly similar*. It reads as follows: "The angel said to her, 'Do not be afraid, Mary, for you have found favor with *God*. And now, you will *conceive* in your womb and *bear a son*, and you will *name Him Jesus* [which means *Savior*]. *He* will be great, and will be called the *Son of the Most High*, and the *Lord God will give to Him the throne of His ancestor David. He will reign* over the house of Jacob <u>*forever*</u>, and of *His Kingdom* there will be <u>no end</u>.' Mary said to the angel, 'How can this be, since I am a *virgin*? The angel said to her, 'The *Holy Spirit* [the *third personality* of *God*] will come upon you, and the *power of the Most High* will overshadow you; therefore the *child* to be born will be *holy*; *He* will be called *Son of God*."

Isaiah also made reference to *the Son* in his forty-fourth chapter where he says, "Thus says the *Lord*, the *King of Israel*, and *His Redeemer*, the *Lord of Hosts*."

Thirdly, the prophet *Hosea* also spoke of *God's Son* in 11:1 of his book. *Hosea* said, "When Israel was a *child*, then I loved him, and *called my son out of Egypt*." (When the *baby Jesus's life was threatened, God, the Father sent Him to Egypt* to protect **Him** from certain death by Herod, the King, and later *God, the Father recalled Him from Egypt* back to Israel when it was safe to come back (Matthew 2:13–15). *Verification that Jesus was being referred to by Hosea* in that above quoted verse is in the last part of verse 15. The verse declares **"that it might be fulfilled* which was spoken of the Lord *by the prophet*, saying, '*Out of Egypt have I called my son*.'"

Lastly, *there is another reference to the divinity of Jesus Christ,* and that is *in the Old Testament book* of *Job. Job* even refers to Him as being resurrected and his personal Savior from the punishment of sin. *Job* proclaims, "I know that my *Redeemer* [meaning *Savior*] liveth, and that **He** shall stand at the latter day upon the earth: and though after my skin, worms destroy this body, yet in my flesh shall I see *God*" (*Job* 19:25).

> I know that my *Redeemer* lives;
> What comfort this sweet sentence gives!
> *He* lives, *He* lives, who once was dead;
> *He* lives, my everliving *head.*
>
> *He* lives, all glory to *His* name!
> *He* lives, my *Jesus,* still the same;
> Oh, the sweet *joy* this sentence gives:
> I know that my *Redeemer* lives!
>
> —Samuel Medley

In summary, *the one and only true God cannot be truly known without the addition of His Son, Jesus Christ.* In *John* 14, *Jesus told* Philip, one of *His* disciples, ***"Believe Me that 'I AM' <u>in the Father and the Father is in Me</u>."*

> *You* are the *Way;* through **You** <u>alone</u>
> Can we the *Father* find;
> In *You,* O *Christ,* has *God* revealed
> *His* heart and will and mind.
>
> *You* are the <u>*Truth*</u>; *Your Word* alone
> *True wisdom* can impart;
> *You only* can *inform* the mind
> And *purify* the heart.

The Third Personality

The *Holy Spirit* is the *third personality* of *God*, mentioned many times in the *New Testament*; one example of which is found in two separate books. Both *Matthew* 1:18 and *Luke* 1:35 record the *conception of Jesus* as coming *from "The Holy Ghost"* (another name for the *Holy Spirit*). A <u>second</u> example is in *John* 4 where it reveals, *"God is a Spirit*: and they that worship *Him* must worship *Him* in *spirit* and in *truth."* A <u>*third*</u> example is in *John* 14, where *Jesus* promised *His* followers, *"I* will pray the *Father*, and *He* shall give you another *Comforter*, that *He* may abide with you *forever*; even the *Spirit of truth."* The <u>*fourth*</u> example is in *Galatians* 5:22, which reads as follows: "But the *fruit of the Spirit* is *love, <u>joy, peace</u>, longsuffering, gentleness, goodness, faith, meekness, temperance, self-control."* This means that if we trust in *Jesus* as our *Savior, He* promises to send us *His Holy Spirit*, enabling us to <u>especially</u> have <u>Joy</u>, and <u>Peace</u>.

The *Holy Spirit* is also mentioned many times in the *Old Testament*. For example, in *Genesis*, the very first book of the *Torah*, it is related that "the *Spirit of God* moved upon the face of the waters" (during the *creation* in 1:2) and later in 6:3, "The *Lord* said, '*My <u>spirit</u>* shall not always strive with man.'" In *Numbers* 11, the <u>*spirit*</u> is mentioned four times, the last of which is in verse 29. In that verse, Moses said, "Would *God* that all the *Lord's* people were prophets, and that the *Lord* would put *his spirit* upon them!" In *Nehemiah* 9:20, the prophet Nehemiah spoke the following: "*Thou* gavest also *thy good spirit* to instruct them, and withheldest not thy manna from their mouth, and gavest them water for their thirst" (speaking of *God's* provisions to the Israelites in the wilderness following their exit from Egypt). King David, in his 104th *Psalm*, also mentioned *God's Spirit* when he said, "*Thou* sendest forth *thy spirit*, they are created: and *thou* renewest the face of the earth" (verse 30).

The whole triumphant host
Give thanks to *God* on high;
"Hail, *Father*, *Son*, and *Holy Ghost*!"
They ever cry.

—Thomas Olivers

Holy Spirit, Joy Divine,
Cheer this saddened heart of mine;
Yield a sacred, settled *Peace*,
Let it grow and still increase

O friends in gladness let us sing,
Supernal anthems echoing:
Alleluia! Alleluia!
To *God* the *Father*, *God the Son*,
And *God the Spirit*, <u>Three</u> in <u>One</u>:
Alleluia, alleluia! Alleluia, alleluia, alleluia!

Chapter 8

The *Tanakh (Old Testament)* is a group of *ancient sacred writings* which set forth *God's definition* of *who* the *Messiah*, the *Savior* from the sins of humankind, would be.

Jesus used the same organization of the *Tanakh* as is used today when *He* made the statement at the beginning of this chapter. *He also said,* *"*Search* the *Scriptures…they* are *they which testify* of *Me*" (*John* 5:39).

According to the great theologian, Dr. D. James Kennedy, the *Old Testament* writings (*Scriptures*) contain over ***333*** *predictions* of the *Messiah whom God* would *send* to *save people* from the *eternal punishment* of *their sins, provided they repented* and *trusted* in *Him* for that *salvation.* Why so many prophecies? So that it wouldn't be missed!

Using the *science* of *probability*, Peter Stoner in *Science Speaks* says that "the *chance* that *any man might have lived down* to the *present time* and have *fulfilled just* 8 of the 333 *prophecies* is 1 in 10 to the 17th *power*." This number has <u>17 zeros</u> in it. ****Yet Jesus Christ perfectly fulfilled God's definition* of who the *Messiah* would be and is the **<u>only one</u>** who has **perfectly fulfilled** all 333 prophecies! Peter Stoner in *Science Speaks* has said that he has provided *numerical evidence* that ****this fulfillment proved Jesus Christ to be the* **Son of God**, *the promised* **Savior**. He even goes so far as to say that ***"*any man who rejects Christ as the Son of God is rejecting a fact proved perhaps more absolutely than any other fact in the world."*

Chapter 9

Jesus said, "This is *My blood* of the *New Covenant*, which
is *shed* for *many* for the *remission (forgiveness)* of *sins*."

—*Matthew* 26:28

The *New Testament* is also called the *"New Covenant"* and for good
reason. The following is the explanation of that reason:

In the *Old Testament*, in *Daniel* 12:2, it says that there will ultimately be a *"Day of Judgment."* This is mentioned in many places in
the *New Testament* as well. One such place is in the ninth chapter
of the letter of Paul to the *Hebrews*, where it says, "It is appointed
unto men once to die, but after this the **_judgment_**." *We are all sinners*
(wrongdoers who have broken God's laws) *in need of forgiveness from
God in order to prevent eternal punishment in a place called "Hell".*
Have you ever done something that was against one of *God's Ten
Commandments?* For example, have you ever lied to someone? The
Bible (God's Word) says in *James* 2:10 that even if we commit only one
sin, we are guilty of them all. The exact words of that verse are as follows: "For whosoever shall keep the whole law, and yet offend in one
point, he is guilty of all." *God is completely holy* (without sin). If *He* is
to remain true to *His* very nature (being completely good and completely just), *He cannot tolerate sin.* As such, *He* can't allow anything
or anyone that is sinful into *His holy heaven* (paradise). You Wouldn't
Want a *God* Who is **Not Just,** Would You? Our sinful condition was
revealed long ago in several of the *Old Testament* books—in *Jeremiah*
17;9–10, in *Ecclesiastes* 7:20, in *Isaiah* 59:2, and in *Isaiah* 64:6. In the
verses noted in *Jeremiah*, it tells us that *God* searches the heart and
He knows that the human heart is "deceitful above all things, and

desperately wicked." In the verse listed in *Ecclesiastes*, it says, "For *there is <u>not</u> a **just** *man* upon earth, that doeth good, and <u>sinneth not</u>.*" Isaiah the prophet said in Chapter 59:2, "But your iniquities (sins or wrongdoings) have separated between you and your *God*, and your sins have hid **His** face from you, that **He** will not hear." Again, in *Isaiah* 64:6, *Isaiah* mentioned, "But we are all as an unclean thing, and all our righteousnesses are as filthy rags." That means that *even our best works are still considered unclean in God's sight. Therefore, we cannot possibly be saved from eternal punishment in "Hell" by simply doing good works.*

<u>*There must be another "Way!"*</u> **To find that "Way" keep reading.**

"Hell" is a real place of everlasting torment! It is mentioned in both the *Old and New Testaments*. In the *Old Testament*, in *Daniel* 12:2, it is revealed that "many of them that sleep in the dust of the earth shall awake, some to everlasting life, and some to shame and everlasting contempt." In the *New Testament*, in *2 Peter* 2:9, it declares, *"The Lord knoweth how to deliver the godly out of temptation, and to reserve the unjust unto the <u>day</u> of <u>judgment</u> to be punished."* According to radio and television evangelist *John **F.** MacArthur **Jr.**, "<u>No</u> <u>one</u> in Scripture spoke more of judgment than Jesus."* He warned about "**hell**" many times. An extremely vivid example is one in which *Luke*, one of *Jesus's* followers, who wrote the book of *Luke* in the *New Testament*, witnessed *Jesus* telling a parable about two separate men, one of which was in *heaven*, and the other in *hell. Jesus* said that the *man in hell was* pleading for himself and also for his worldly (in every sense of the word) family. The man in *hell* "lifted up his eyes, *being in torment,* and cried and said, '*Father Abraham, have mercy on me, and send Lazarus, that he may dip the tip of his finger in water, and <u>cool</u> my tongue; for I am <u>tormented</u> in this flame*" (*Luke* 16). At a separate time, *Jesus* said, "Fear not them which kill the body, but are not able to kill the soul: but rather fear *Him* which is able to destroy both soul and body in *hell*" (*Matthew* 10:28). Another time *He* described "hell" as "the *fire* that never shall be quenched" (*Mark* 9:43). This description of "hell" becomes all the more convincing when one is told the following true accounts: *Reverend Kenneth Hagin* described

his visit to *hell* in "**I** Believe in Visions." He said that at the age of fifteen, he died of a severe heart condition three times in the same day and experienced the same thing each time. He states, "The farther down I went, the blacker it became…and the hotter and more stifling it became. Upon reaching the bottom of the pit, I became conscious of some kind of spirit being by my side. When I paused, that creature laid his hand on my arm to escort me in" (to the *fires of the caverns of the damned*). Hagin's spirit suddenly came back into his body at the command of *God*. After that experience, Rev. Hagin went on to become a *minister* for more than *sixty years*. He also wrote an excerpt about the death of his grandmother's distant cousin. She was definitely <u>not</u> <u>a</u> <u>Christian</u> and *refused to believe in heaven or hell*. On her *deathbed*, she was witnessed as crying, "I'm afraid. It's so dark! *It's so* dark! <u>IT'S SO DARK!</u>"

An even more horrific experience was related by *Bill Wiese* in his book *23 Minutes in Hell.* At 3:00 a.m. one night, he was *chosen by Jesus to experience hell* for a short time, because *Jesus* wanted him to warn us all of its existence. Bill states, "I was catapulted out of my bed into the very pit of hell. My point of arrival was a cell with walls of rough stone and rigid bars on the door." (In *Isaiah* 24:22 of the *Old Testament* Scriptures, it says, "And they shall be gathered together, as prisoners are gathered in the pit, and shall be shut up in the prison.") As I lay there on the floor, I felt extremely weak. I saw two enormous beasts unlike anything I had ever seen before. They were entirely evil, and they were gazing at me with pure, unrestrained hatred, which completely paralyzed me with fear. Suddenly, the light vanished. It became absolutely pitch black. One of the creatures picked me up. The beast threw me against the wall. I felt as though every bone in my body had been broken. The second beast plunged his claws into my chest, and my flesh hung from my body like ribbons. I was so extremely nauseous from the terrible stench coming from these creatures. There was no humidity or moisture in the air. I was so extremely thirsty. It was exhausting to try to get just one breath. In hell, you never sleep, rest, or find a quiet moment. There is never any peace of mind. To have any conversation with a human being was completely unattainable. The fact that I knew *God* was kept from my mind. The mental anguish I felt was indescribable.

Now I found myself next to an enormous pit with raging flames of fire leaping high into an open cavern. (In *Psalm* 140:10, we read, "Let burning coals fall upon them: let them be cast into the fire; into deep pits, that they rise not up again.") I was horrified as I heard the screams of an untold multiple of people, crying out in torment. I saw many people reaching out of the pit of fire, desperately trying to claw their way out. But there was no way out. I realized this horror would last for an eternity.

Suddenly, a burst of *light* invaded the entire tunnel. It was so bright that I could not even see the face of the one who was before me, but I instantly knew who *He* was. I said, "***Jesus***," and *He* said, "***I AM***" (signifying that *He* was *God Himself*), and I fell at *His* feet. Fortunately for Bill, the torment did end, but he has been tirelessly warning others ever since. He declared, "We must get the truth out to people so they can know that there is a choice to make. **Without Jesus** as your **Savior**, you will **not** be going to **heaven**, and that is absolutely **certain**."

****Fortunately,* God also revealed **His provision** for **forgiveness** of *our sins* (atonement) in *Leviticus* 17:11. It is found there that "it is the **blood** that maketh an **atonement** for the **soul**." Since the destruction of the Jewish temple in AD 70, *there have not been blood sacrifices* of goats, bulls, or rams as specified in *Leviticus* 16. It is clear that *forgiveness of our sins is not possible without a **blood sacrifice**.* How then can we get forgiveness today if blood sacrifices are not made today? *In the Old Testament book of Jeremiah* 31:31–34, **God** promised a **New Covenant** (New Testament—sacred agreement and promise) indicating that *God* was going to do something for us. *God* said, "Behold, the days come, saith the *Lord*, that I will make a *new covenant* [testament] with the house of Israel, and with the house of Judah: *not* according to the covenant [testament] that I *made with their fathers* …the day that *I* took them by the hand to bring them out of the land of Egypt: which *My covenant* they brake, although *I* was an husband unto them, saith the *Lord*: But this shall be the *covenant (testament)* that *I* will make with the house of Israel; After those days, saith the Lord, *I* will put *my* law in their inward parts, and write it in their hearts; and will be their *God*, and *they shall be my* people. And they shall teach no more every man his neighbor, and every man his brother, saying, "Know the *Lord*": for *they shall all know Me*, from the least of them unto the greatest of them, saith the *Lord*: for *I will forgive their iniquity*, (sin) and *I* will remember their sin no more."

***God** had stated *his* _final_ and most important _provision_, and this is of *foremost* and *utmost* importance in *regard* to the eternal *salvation* of *our souls*. In those verses, *God indicated* that the *old covenant* (**testament**) made at Mt. Sinai **would become obsolete,** would be of a temporary nature only, and a *new covenant* (**New Testament**) *would be made*. It is written in *Matthew* 26:28 that *Jesus*, during *His* last supper with the twelve disciples before *His* terribly *brutal crucifixion*, (lifted His chalice) and *stated*, ***"*This* is *My blood* of the **New Testament (Covenant)** which is *shed for many* for the *remission* of *sins*." This is *substantiated in Mark* 14:24, in *Luke* 22:20, and in *1 Corinthians* 11:25 where it is recorded that *Jesus* said _essentially_ _the_ _same_ _thing_.

It is also very clearly stated in *Hebrews* 12:24 that the **New Covenant* (**New Testament***) involves Jesus.* The verse begins, "And to *Jesus the mediator* of the *New Covenant (Testament)*." It is completely explained in the entire eighth chapter of *Hebrews.* Here we even find the verse in *Jeremiah,* chapter 31 (as previously listed) that deals with this very subject.

In God's "New Covenant (**New Testament Holy Scriptures / Bible***)," He did indeed make a special provision for us for the forgiveness of our sins. He* tells us in *John* 3:16, "*God* so loved the world that *He* gave *His* only begotten *Son,* that whosoever believeth in *Him* should not perish, but have everlasting life." *He carried out His great plan of sending a* **Messiah** *(a* **Savior***)—His formula for salvation, open-ing up the* <u>pathway</u> *to heaven to those who would repent and believe.* <u>*He arranged for*</u> *that one vital,* ***<u>*necessary blood sacrifice*</u> *by allow-ing His one and only Son to come down to the earth for thirty-three years to live as a sinless human being (thereby obeying the Law [the Ten Commandments] for us), and then putting all our punishment on that Son by finally sacrificing that Son on a crucifixion tree.*

God allowed His Son's precious blood to be shed in order to save <u>**us**</u> *from eternal punishment.* Anyone who has lost a child to death can certainly understand what a great sacrifice that must have been. Both *God, the Father,* and *His Son, Jesus,* must have had ***extreme love for us*** in order to carry out that most compassionate of all plans.

Evangelist *John F. MacArthur Jr.,* in his book *The Murder of Jesus,* described what the *Lord Jesus* must have suffered (both physically and mentally) at the hands of the cruel Roman soldiers during *His* execution. *He* was taunted and made fun of in front of hundreds of soldiers and civilians, slapped in the face, scourged, and beaten repeatedly. *His* face was undoubtedly swollen and bleeding, and *His* back would be a mass of bleeding wounds and quivering muscles because of the Roman scourging. The *crown of thorns* that they fashioned contained "no doubt" the *longest, sharpest thorns that could be found.*

It is recorded in *Mark 15:19 and Matthew 27:30* that one of the soldiers took a reed and smote Him on His head to *inflict great pain on His already battered head (page 192).* **Jesus Christ** would have been nailed to the cross as it lay flat on the ground. The nails had to be *driven through the wrists, because neither the tendons nor the bone structure in the hands could support the body's weight.* As the *nail* went into the *wrist,* it would usually cause *severe damage* to the *sensorimotor* median *nerve,* causing *intense pain* in *both arms.* Finally, a single nail would be driven through both feet. *The nail wounds would all cause intense and increasing pain.* Soldiers would elevate the top of the cross and it would *drop* with a *jarring blow* into the *bottom* of the *hole,* causing the *full weight* of the victim (*Jesus*) to be immediately *borne* by the *nails* in the wrists and feet. That would cause a *bone-wrenching pain* throughout the *whole body, as major joints were suddenly twisted out of their natural position. *This was all predicted in Psalm 22 of the Old Testament,* which says, "*I* am poured out like water, and all My bones are out of joint" *(verse 14).* The Romans had perfected the art of crucifixion in order to *maximize the pain*, and they knew how to *prolong the horror without permitting* the victim to lapse into *unconsciousness. Jesus would have experienced waves of nausea, fever, intense thirst, constant cramps, and incessant, throbbing pain from all parts of His body, sleeplessness, hunger, dehydration, and worsening infection.* "*Because of the cramps in His muscles and the fatigue, Jesus would have had to fight to raise Himself in order to get even one short breath. Ultimately fatigue, intense pain, or muscle atrophy would render **Him** unable to do this, and He would finally die from the lack of oxygen. **Jesus** **love**s **us** so much that **He** **was** **willing** to* suffer all this *constant* and prolonged physical agony *and* not only that. ***He*** suffered horrendous **spiritual agony** *because He took on all the* **punishment** *that* **we** **deserve**—*the terrible loneliness and unspeakable torments of* "***hell***" itself. ***He*** *is indeed the* long-awaited **Messiah** *sent by God, the Father in His* **New Covenant (New Testament)** *as stated in the Old Testament (Tanakh)_in Jeremiah* 31:31–34: ***In His New*** **Testament** *(Covenant), God forgives all of our sins and* "*remembers them no more*" *so that we may obtain the promise of eternal life in heaven (Hebrews 9:15). Jesus died as a ransom to set us free from sins committed.* We need only to *admit* that we are *sinners, repent* of our sins to ***Jesus***, *ask* for *His forgiveness,* live a *new life* for ***Him***, (sincerely trying to *obey **His*** commands) and put our full and *complete trust* in *Him* for *salvation from* the *punishment* of our *sins.*

> There is a fountain filled with blood
> Drawn from *Immanuel's veins*
> And sinners plunged beneath that flood
> Lose all their guilty stains.
>
> Dear dying *Lamb, Thy* precious blood
> Shall never lose its pow'r,
> Till all the ransomed *Church of God*
> *Be saved* to sin no more.
>
> —William Cowper

Chapter 10

They shall call *His* name *Immanuel*
(meaning "*God* with us").

—*Isaiah* 7:14 and *Matthew* 1:23

A large number of the *same words* appear in both the *Old* and *New Testament*, thereby indicating that the* *second set of scrolls* is indeed *a perfect fulfillment of the first.*

The <u>first</u> example of this appears in both *Isaiah* 7:14 of the *Old Testament* and in *Matthew* 1:23 of the *New Testament*. The *words are the same*, namely, "Behold a *virgin* shall be with child, and shall bring forth a *son*, and they shall call his name *Immanuel*, which being interpreted is, *God with us*." In the *Isaiah* verse, the words are preceded by, "Behold the *Lord* shall give you a <u>*sign*</u>," and in the *Matthew* verse, the words are preceded by "And she shall bring forth a *Son*, and thou shalt call *His* name *Jesus*: for *He* shall save *His* people from their sins." The name *Immanuel* is one of the many names for *Jesus* in the *Bible*. And because *Immanuel means "God with us,"* it is clear that the name "*Immanuel*" refers to *Jesus*. <u>*He is*</u>, therefore, the <u>*second personality of God Himself*</u>. Not only that—the name "*Jesus*" literally means "*Savior*."

The **second** example of the *same prophetical words* occurs in *Psalm* 22:18 (from the *Old Testament*). There it states, "They *part my garments* among them, and *cast lots upon my* vesture." *Practically, the same words appear in Luke* 23:34 (from the *New Testament*). These are, "And they *parted His raiment*, and *cast lots*." The same prophetical words are *also seen in Mark* (from the *New Testament*) in 15:24 in which this event in the life of *Jesus* on earth is recorded as, "And when they had crucified *Him, they parted **His** garments, casting lots* upon them, what each man should take." The same words are *also seen in Matthew 27:35 (New Testament)*, in which it states, "And they crucified *Him*, and *parted **His** garments, casting lots.*"

The **third** example of the *same words in both sets of scrolls* is as follows: In *Psalms* 2:1, it is stated, *"My God, my God, why hast thou forsaken me?"* **Jesus** cried out the very same words to *His Father in heaven* when *He* was dying in great agony on the crucifixion tree. This is recorded in *Mark* 15:34 as, "And at the ninth hour *Jesus* cried with a loud voice, saying, "Eloi, Eloi, la ma sa-bach-tha-ni?" Which is, being interpreted, '*My God, My God, Why Hast Thou Forsaken Me?*' The very same thing is recorded in *Matthew* 27:46 as, "And about the ninth hour *Jesus cried* with a loud voice, saying, Eli, Eli, la ma sa-bach-tha-ni?" That is to say, *"My God, My God, Why Hast Thou Forsaken Me?" Jesus, in His agony, uttered these words because He was suffering in our stead, the torment of "hell" where there is complete and utter absence of God.*

The **fourth** example of the *same words* appearing in both *Old Testament* and *New Testament* is the following: In *Psalm* 22:8, it states, *"He trusted on the Lord… Let him deliver him."* During *Jesus's* crucifixion, it is stated in *Matthew* 27:43 that *He* was *mocked* by these same words: *"He* trusted in *God… Let Him* deliver *Him."*

The **fifth** example of the same words in both sets of scrolls is the following: In *Isaiah* 53:5, it states, "And *with his stripes we are healed."* In the *New Testament*, this appears in *1 Peter* 2:24 as, *"By whose stripes ye were healed."* This was preceded by, "*Christ* also suffered for us, leaving us an example, that ye should follow *His* steps: *who* did no sin, neither was guile in *His* mouth: *who* when *He* was reviled, reviled not again; when *He* suffered, *He* threatened not; but committed *Himself* to *Him* that judgeth righteously; *who His* own self bare our sins in *His* own body on the tree, that we, being dead to sins, should live unto righteousness."

The **sixth** example is one in which *two sets* of *words are essentially* the *same words used* in *both Old* and *New Testaments*. The *New Testament* verses in *Galatians* 3 explain the meaning of *two separate* *prophecies taken from the Old Testament book of Genesis.* One prophecy was from *Genesis* 12:3 in which it was stated by *God* to Abraham, "In thee shall all families of the earth be blessed," and the other prophecy was also from *Genesis* 3:15, in which it was stated that *God* spoke to the devil inside the serpent, saying, "I will put enmity between thee and the woman [Eve] and between thy *seed* and her seed." The meaning of the *first* of these prophecies is revealed in The *New Testament,* in *Galatians* 3:8. It states, "And the *Scripture, foreseeing that God would justify the heathen through faith,* preached the good news of salvation through *Christ]* (*Jesus*) unto *Abraham,* saying, 'In thee (meaning through his descendant, *Jesus*) shall *all nations* be *blessed.*'" The meaning of the *second* of these prophecies is also in *Galatians.* In 3:16 of that book, it says, "Now *to Abraham and his seed were the promises made.* He saith not, And to seeds, as of many; but as of *one,* and to thy seed which is Christ." In addition, verses 11–13, 19, 22–24, 26, and 28–29 in *Galatians* 3 stress *the very essence of salvation.* They say, "*No man* is *justified by the law* in the *sight of God,* it is evident: for, *the just shall live by faith.* And the law is not of faith... *Christ* hath redeemed us from the *curse* of the *law,* being made a curse for us...wherefore then serveth the law? It was added because of transgressions, (sins) *till the seed should come* to whom the promise was made...but the *Scripture* hath concluded all under sin, that *the promise by faith of Jesus Christ might be given to them that believe.* But before faith came, we were kept under the law, shut up unto the faith which should afterwards be revealed. Wherefore the law was our schoolmaster to bring us unto *Christ,* that we might be *justified by faith...* For ye are all the children of *God* by *faith* in *Christ Jesus...* There is neither Jew nor Greek...for ye are all *one* in *Christ Jesus.* And if ye be *Christ's,* then are ye Abraham's seed, and heirs according to the promise."

> Blest be the tie that binds
> Our hearts in *Christian love*!
> The fellowship of kindred minds
> Is like to that above.

> —John Fawcett

Chapter 11

Jesus said to the multitudes, "Think not that
I AM come to destroy the law, or the prophets:
I AM not come to destroy, but *to fulfil*."

—*Matthew* 5:17

There are many examples of places in the *New Testament* where it is even *indicated* in the *Scripture* verses that *fulfillments of the prophecies* from the *Old Testament are taking place*. Several of these are as follows:

<u>*The first*</u> and <u>*most significant*</u> example is located in *Luke* 4:16–21. It reads as follows: "*He [Jesus]* went into the synagogue on the Sabbath day, and stood up for to read. And there was delivered unto *Him* the book of the prophet Esaias [*Isaiah*]. And when *He* had opened the book, *He* found the place where it was written, 'The *Spirit of the Lord* is *upon me*, because *the Lord* hath *anointed me* to preach the gospel [the good news] to the poor; *he* hath sent *me* to heal the brokenhearted, to preach deliverance to the captives, and recovering of sight to the blind, to set at liberty them that are bruised, to preach the acceptable year of the *Lord*' [see **Isaiah 61**]. And *He* closed the book, and *He* gave it again to the minister, and sat down. And the eyes of all them that were in the synagogue were fastened on *Him*. And *He began* to *say* unto them, **"*This DAY* is *this Scripture fulfilled* in *your ears*.'"

Hark the _glad_ sound! The _Savior_ comes
The _Savior_ promised long
Let ev'ry heart prepare a throne
And ev'ry voice a song

_He_ comes the pris'ners to release
In Satan's bondage held
The gates of brass before _Him_ burst
The iron fetters yield

_He_ comes the broken heart to bind
The bleeding soul to cure
And with the treasures of _His_ grace
To enrich the humble poor

Our _glad_ hosannas, _Prince of Peace_
Thy welcome shall proclaim
And heav'n's eternal arches ring
With _Thy_ beloved name

The second example appears in the _New Testament_, in _Matthew_ 1:22, where it states, "Now all this was done, *that it might be fulfilled which was spoken of the _Lord_ by the prophet _Isaiah_, saying, 'Behold, a virgin shall be with child, and shall bring forth a son, and they shall call his name _Emmanuel_,' which being interpreted is _God with us_ (from _Isaiah_ 7:14). This statement of fulfillment was preceded in verse 21 of _Matthew's_ first chapter by, "And she shall bring forth a _Son_, and thou shalt call _His_ name _Jesus_: for **H**e _shall save His people_ from _their sins_."

The third example is found in the _New Testament_, in _Matthew_ 2:23 where it states, "And _He_ came and dwelt in a city called _Nazareth_: *that it might be fulfilled which was spoken by the prophets, '_He [Jesus]_ shall be called a _Nazarene_.'"

The fourth example regarding prophecy fulfillment is located in _Matthew_ 11:7 and 10. It is here that _Jesus said that John the Baptist_ (the forerunner of Jesus who announced that _Jesus_, the _Messiah_, was about to come to the people) *was the person spoken of in* the *Old Testament* in *Malachi* 3:1. Theses verses read as follows: "*Jesus* began to say to the multitudes concerning John… *'For this is he of whom it is written, *Behold, I send my messenger before thy face, which shall prepare thy (Jesus's) way before thee.*'" The entire verse in *Malachi* is the following: "Behold, *I* will send of whom it is written, *my* messenger, and he shall prepare the way before *me*: and the *Lord*, whom ye seek, *shall suddenly come to <u>his</u> <u>temple</u>*, even the *messenger* of the *Covenant*, whom ye delight in: behold *he* shall come, saith the *Lord of Hosts*."

Jesus was in the temple at twelve years of age, teaching the people and explaining the meaning of the *Scriptures*. This is found in *Luke* 2:42, 46, and 47, where it states, "And when *He* was twelve years old, they went up to *Jerusalem* after the custom of the feast. And when they had fulfilled the days, as they returned, the *child Jesus* tarried behind in *Jerusalem* and *they found Him in the temple*, sitting in the midst of the doctors, both hearing them, and asking them questions…and all that heard *Him* were *astonished* at *His understanding* and answers." In the same chapter, in verse 49, it is revealed that *Jesus* later asked *His* parents, "How is it that ye sought *Me*? Wist ye not that *I must be about My Father's business?*" (*God, His Heavenly Father's business*).

The fifth example of *spoken words* of *fulfillment* of the *Old Testament is revealed* in not only one, but *two books of the New Testament*. The *first is Matthew* 13:13–15. Here it states that *Jesus* said, "Therefore speak *I* to them [*the Jews*] in parables: because *they seeing see not*: and *hearing they hear not, neither do they understand*. *And *in them is fulfilled the prophecy of Esaias* [*Isaiah*] which saith, 'By hearing ye *shall hear*, and *shall not understand*; and seeing ye shall see, and *shall not perceive*.'" *Jesus* goes on to say, "For the heart of this people has grown dull. Their ears are hard of hearing, and their eyes they have closed, lest they should see with their eyes and hear with their ears, *lest they should understand with their heart and turn so that I should heal them*."

The <u>*second place*</u> in the *New Testament* where these <u>same words</u> <u>appear</u> together with an indication that they appeared in *earlier Scripture* is in the Epistle of Paul the apostle to the *Romans*, in 11:5–

8. It reads as follows: "Even so then at this present time also *there is a remnant* according to the election of grace [*salvation as a gift of God through belief and trust in Jesus Christ*]…if by grace, then is it no more of works: otherwise grace is no longer grace… Israel hath not obtained that which he seeketh for; but the election hath obtained it, and *the rest* were *blinded* (according as it is written, *God* hath given them the spirit of slumber, eyes that they should not see, and ears that they should not hear; unto this day…and David [the King] saith, 'Let their eyes be darkened, that they may not see'" (Psalm 69:23). In *Isaiah* 44:18, it states the *same words*, namely, that "they [the Jews] have not known nor understood: for *he* hath shut their eyes, that they cannot see; and their hearts, that they cannot understand." These *very same words are repeated again* in *Isaiah* 6:9–10 as follows: "Keep on hearing, but do not understand; keep on seeing, but do not perceive. Make the heart of this people dull, and their ears heavy, and shut their eyes; *lest they* see with their eyes, and hear with their ears, and understand with their heart, and *return and be healed.*"

In verses 34 and 35 of the same chapter of *Matthew* listed above, there occurs *a second statement of prophecy fulfillment*. It states, namely, "All these things <u>spake</u> *Jesus* unto the multitude <u>*in*</u> <u>*parables*</u>; and without a parable spake *He* not unto them: **That it might be fulfilled which was spoken by the prophet, saying, I will open my mouth <u>in parables</u>; I will utter things which have been kept secret from the foundation of the world.*" *The Old Testament prophecy* to which Jesus was referring is found in *Psalm* 78:2. Here it states, *"I will open my mouth in a parable: I will utter dark sayings of old."*

The sixth example is located in *Matthew* 8:16–17. It reads as follows: "When the even was come, they brought unto *Him [Jesus]* many that were possessed with devils: and *He* cast out the spirits with *His* Word, and *healed* all that were sick: **that it might be fulfilled which was spoken by Esaias [Isaiah] the prophet*, saying, 'Himself took our infirmities, and bare our sicknesses.'" You recall that same statement in *Isaiah* 53:4–5 in which Isaiah says, "Surely he hath borne our griefs, and carried our sorrows…*with his stripes, we are healed.*"

The seventh example occurred at the Last Supper that *Jesus* had with *His* disciples before *His* arrest. It is written in *Matthew* 26:31, where *Jesus* states, "All ye shall be offended because of *Me* this night: *for it is written*, I will *smite the shepherd*, and the *sheep* of the flock shall be *scattered abroad*," prophesied in *Zechariah 13:7 (Old Testament)*.

The eighth example occurs in *Matthew* 27:35. Here it reads as follows: "And they crucified *Him* [meaning *Jesus*], and *parted His garments, casting lots*: *that it might be fulfilled* which was spoken by the prophet." "They *parted my garments* among them, and upon *my* vesture did they *cast lots*" (*Psalm* 22:18).

The ninth example concerns an event during *Jesus's* crucifixion. *Psalm* 69:21 states as follows: "They gave *me* also *gall* for *my* meat; and in *my* thirst they gave *me vinegar to drink*." *This is stated as being fulfilled in John* 19:28–29 *(New Testament)* where it is recorded that "*Jesus* knowing that all things were now accomplished, *that the Scripture might be fulfilled, saith, '*I* thirst.' Now there was set a vessel full of vinegar: and *they filled a sponge with vinegar*, and put it upon hyssop, and *put it to His mouth*."

The tenth example is an instance in which it is actually stated in the *New Testament that another prophecy from the Old Testament has been fulfilled*. In *John* 19:33–37, the following is revealed: "When they [the soldiers] came to *Jesus, they brake <u>not</u> His legs* (a common practice at that time was to break the legs of all crucified victims): But one of the soldiers with a *spear* <u>pierced</u> *His side*, and forthwith came there out blood and water. And he that saw it bare record, and his *record is* <u>true</u>: and he knoweth that he said <u>true</u>, *that ye might believe. For these things were done, *that the Scripture should be fulfilled* [from *Psalm 34:20*], 'A bone of him shall not be broken.'* And again *another Scripture saith,* 'They shall look *on him whom they* <u>pierced</u>'" (from *Zechariah* 12:10).

The eleventh example shows *not only one statement of prophecy fulfillment but two* statements that occur *in the same group of verses*. This is found in *Matthew* 26:50, and 52–56. Theses verses say the following: "Then came they, and laid hands on *Jesus*, and took *Him*… Then said *Jesus*… Thinkest thou that *I* cannot now pray to *My Father* and *He* shall presently give *Me* more than twelve legions [about seventy-two thousand according to page 793 of the *Bible Commentary New Testament Volume 2*) of angels? *But how then shall the Scriptures* *be fulfilled, that thus it must be?* In that same hour said *Jesus* to the multitude, Are ye come out as against a thief with swords and staves for to take *Me*? *I* sat daily with you teaching in the temple, and ye laid no hand on **Me**. **But all this was done, that the Scriptures of the prophets might be fulfilled.*"

The twelfth example occurs in *John* 18:8–9. It is read as follows: "*Jesus* answered, 'I have told you that *I AM **He***: if therefore ye seek **Me**, let these go their way.' **That the saying might be fulfilled, which **He** [Jesus] spake*, 'Of them which **Thou** gavest **Me** have *I lost none.*'" *Jesus* had spoken these same words earlier as **He** had prayed to *His Heavenly Father*, saying, "Those that **Thou** gavest **Me** *I* have kept, and *none of them is lost*, but the son of perdition [Judas, *His* betrayer] **that the **Scripture** might be fulfilled*" (related in *John* 17:12).

The thirteenth example *is* recorded in *John* 15:25. The context is as follows: *Jesus* had just told *His* followers in verse 18 that "if the world hate you, ye know that it hated *Me* before it hated you." And in verse 23 that "he that hateth *Me* hateth *My Father* also." Then follows the statement of fulfillment in verse 25 as *Jesus* related, "But *this cometh to pass, *that the Word might be fulfilled that is written in their law, 'They hated me without a cause*" (*prophesied* in *ancient* times in *Psalm* 69:4).

> No work is left undone
> Of all the *Father* willed;
> *His* toil, *His* sorrows, one by one,
> The *Scriptures have fulfilled.*

> —Henry W. Baker

Another cover page containing the following song:

Lo, how a *Rose* e'er blooming
From tender stem hath sprung!
Of Jesse's lineage coming
As *men of old* have sung.

It came, a *flow'r-et* bright,
Amid the cold of winter,
When half spent was the night.

Isaiah 'twas foretold it,
The *Rose* I have in mind,
With *Mary* we behold *it,*
The *Virgin Mother* kind.

To shew (show) *God's love* a-right
She bore to men a *Savior,*
When half spent was the night.

"I AM" the Rose of Sharon (It's **Jesus**!!)

Song of Solomon 2:1

John declared in the fourteenth chapter of his book that *Jesus* comforted *His* followers with the words, "Do not let your hearts be troubled… *I AM* the *Way,* the *Truth,* and the *Life*" (now and eternally). *When Jesus said the words "I AM" in that verse, He was proclaiming that He is God (God's second personality).* This is very significant because in the *Old Testament* in the book of *Exodus,* in 3:14–15, *God had revealed His name as "I AM." He* had told Moses, "I AM THAT I AM." And *He* had then commanded Moses to say unto the children of Israel (the Jewish people), "'*I AM*' hath sent me unto you." *God* had even declared, "This is *My name forever,* and this is *my* memorial unto all generations." *Jesus was saying that "as God," He Himself was the "Way" to heaven, the "Truth," and the "Life" now and forever,* and that *His* followers could have complete confidence in *Him* for their present life and for their life after physical death (eternity). *He was giving them "peace" and "joy"* in their hearts, dispelling their fear of death. *Jesus* frequently used the name *"I AM"* in *His* entire ministry as we will see.

On another occasion, *Jesus <u>promised</u>* them that after *His* ascension back into heaven, *He would <u>send</u> to them <u>His</u> <u>Holy</u> <u>Spirit</u> (God's third personality). He* said, "When *He,* the *Spirit of truth,* comes, *He* will guide you into all *truth*…and *He* will tell you what is yet to come" *(John* 16:13). The *Holy Spirit* did indeed come to *His* followers at *"Pentecost,"* according to the *New Testament* book of *Acts,* in 2:4.

Chapter 12

In the beginning was the *Word*, and the *Word*
was with *God*, and the *Word was God.*

—John 1:1

And the *Word* *was made flesh*
and *dwelt among us.*

—John 1:14

In order to satisfy *God the Father's requirements for saving us from eternal
punishment by the shedding of His own blood, Jesus needed* to have both a
human nature and a *divine nature.* This is illustrated completely in the
above *Bible* passages. The apostle Paul stressed that same concept as he
wrote to the *Romans*, in 8:3. He says, "For what the law could not do,
in that it was weak through the flesh, *God* sending *His own Son in the
likeness of human flesh*, and for sin, condemned sin in the flesh."

St Paul also mentioned the same thing in his letter to the
Philippians when he wrote about *Jesus*, saying, "And took upon *Him*
the form of a servant, and was *made in the likeness of men*" (2:7).
Again, in his epistle to the *Colossians* 2:9, Paul told them, "For in
Him [*Jesus Christ*] dwelleth all the fullness of *the Godhead bodily.*"

Jesus's miraculous conception testifies to His being both God and Man.
St. *Matthew* recorded that "when as *His mother Mary* [a *human* woman]
was espoused to Joseph, before they came together [she was a *virgin*], she
was found with *child of the Holy Ghost* [Holy Spirit]" (*Matthew* 1:18).
This same miraculous act was confirmed in *Luke* 1, where it is *recorded*
that an *angel* told *Mary*, "The *Holy Ghost* (Holy Spirit) shall come upon

thee, and the *power of the Highest* shall overshadow thee: therefore also that **holy** thing which shall be born of thee shall be called the "**Son of God.**"

In two separate events of *Jesus's* life, *His Heavenly Father testified of Jesus's divinity*. The first event occurred during *Jesus's* baptism by *John the Baptist*. St. *Matthew* related this scene in 3:16–17 as he stated the following: "*Jesus*, when *He* was baptized, went up straightway out of the water: and lo, the *heavens were opened unto Him*, and *He* saw the *Spirit of God* descending like a dove, and lighting upon *Him*: and lo a *voice from heaven*, saying, '*This is My beloved Son*, in *whom* "*I AM*" well pleased." In the second event, *Jesus's transfiguration* (change of appearance into radiant glory) occurred on a high mountain and was *witnessed* by Peter, James, and John. They saw that "*His face did shine* as the sun, and *His raiment* was <u>white as the light</u>." *Jesus again heard His Heavenly Father's voice*. This is related to us in the following words: "While he [Peter] yet spake, Behold, a *bright cloud* overshadowed them: and behold a *voice out of the cloud*, which said, '*This is My beloved Son, in whom* "*I AM*" well pleased; hear ye *Him*" (*Matthew* 17:5).

Jesus also said of *Himself*, ***"Before Abraham was "I AM""* (recorded in *John* 8:58). *Jesus* spoke to *His Father* at one point, say-ing, "And now, O *Father*, <u>glorify</u> <u>Thou</u> <u>Me</u> with Thine own self <u>with the glory which I had with Thee before the world was</u>" (*John* 17:5) and "*Holy Father*, keep through *Thine* own name those whom *Thou* hast given *Me*, ***that they may be <u>one, as We are</u>*" (verse 11).

St. Paul, in his epistle to the *Hebrews, testified that **Jesus is both God's Son and God Himself** when he wrote, ***"But unto the **Son** He (God) saith, "Thy throne, O **God**, is forever and ever." (Hebrews* 1:8). **God the Father** *is showing that **His Son is "God." (<u>the second personality</u> <u>of</u> <u>God</u>)***

In his first letter to *Timothy*, the apostle Paul related very clearly that "without controversy *great* is the *mystery of godliness: God* was manifest *in the flesh*, justified in the *Spirit*, seen of angels, *preached* unto the Gentiles, *believed on* in the world, *received up into glory*" (3:16). ***Jesus was truly both God and Man.***

Jesus said, ***"Believe Me that "I AM" in the Father, and the Father in Me." (*John* 14:11)

Chapter 13

Jesus said, "Foxes have holes, and birds of the air have nests: but the *Son of Man* hath not where to lay *His* head."

—*Luke* 9:58

Having been born of the *virgin Mary* (as recorded in *Matthew* 1), *Jesus* took on *His human nature*. Moreover, *Jesus*, at times, called *Himself* the *Son of Man* because *He* needed to be able to show us that *He could identify with us as human beings* in all aspects. We can, therefore, know that *Jesus knew what it was like to have both human physical pain and human emotional pain.*

Jesus had all the physical attributes of being human. One such attribute was that of *growth*. As a human child, *Jesus* "grew, and waxed strong in *spirit*" (*Luke* 2:40).

Another set of human attributes was that of *hunger and thirst*. In *Luke* 4:1–2, it says, "And *Jesus*…was led by the *Spirit* into the wilderness, being forty days tempted of the devil. And in those days *He* did eat nothing: and when they were ended, *He* afterward hungered." When *Jesus* was being crucified, *He* said, *"I thirst"* (*John* 19:28).

A third attribute was that of *weariness*. Just as we become weary, *He* also became weary at times. The apostle *John* mentioned one of those times in 4:6 as follows: "*Jesus*, therefore, being wearied with *His* journey, sat thus on the well." *He* even became so tired that *He* fell asleep in a boat as recorded in *Luke* 8:23. This reads, "As they sailed, *He* fell asleep."

Jesus personally experienced all the emotions that we, as humans, feel. For example, we find in the book of *Matthew* that *Jesus suffered being tempted*, just as we are tempted (4:1–10). *Matthew* recorded that after being in the wilderness for forty days and forty nights, *Jesus had been tempted by the devil three times*. The devil even quoted a *Bible* passage from *Psalm* 91 to try to trick *Jesus* into submitting to him. First, he took *Jesus* to a very high part of the *temple* and said, "If *Thou* be the *Son of God* [he knew that *Jesus* was the *Son of God*], cast *Thyself* down: for it is written [in the *Holy Scriptures*], '*He* shall give *His* angels charge concerning *Thee*: and in their hands they shall bear *Thee* up, lest *Thou* dash *Thy* foot against a stone.'" *Jesus, being God*, didn't fall for Satan's deception. *He* is much more powerful than the devil. *He overcame the temptations by quoting the Holy Scriptures*, saying, "Get thee hence, Satan, for it is written, 'Thou shalt worship the *Lord* thy *God*, and *Him* <u>only</u> shalt thou serve.'" How *Jesus* overcame temptations by the devil serves as *a lesson to us on how to flee from sin. Jesus* tells us (in the *Holy Scriptures*) that *the devil is* "a <u>liar</u>, and the father of it" (*John* 8:44). He will use anything at his disposal to try to trick and deceive you. For example, he will use witchcraft (including the use of horoscopes, palm reading, and Ouija boards), illegal drugs, and alcohol or anything else to cause you to forget about *Jesus* and disobey *Him*.

In 1 *Samuel* 15:23, the prophet *Samuel* tells Saul that "rebellion is as the sin of witchcraft." St. Paul, the apostle, tells the *Galatians* in chapter 5 not to walk in the works of the flesh (witchcraft, drunkenness, fornication, etc.) but to walk in the *Spirit* (love, <u>*Joy*</u>, <u>*Peace*</u>, longsuffering, gentleness, goodness, faith, meekness, temperance). Remember that *God's laws* (The Ten Commandments) are *there* to *protect you* from *physical* and *emotional "pain." Don't* give in to Satan. He will make your life miserable, and *you will lose your God-given* "<u>joy</u>" and "<u>peace</u>." *Pray to Jesus when you are tempted* and *use God's Word to combat it.*

In *James* 4, it says, "Resist the devil, and he will flee from you." How *Jesus* won the victory serves as *an example* as to how we too can combat temptation, no matter how tempting the devil can make it. *Hebrews* 2:18 states, "For in that *He [Jesus] Himself* hath suffered being tempted, *He is able to succor (help) them that are tempted.*"

Have we trials and temptations?
Is there trouble anywhere?
We should never be discouraged
Take it to the Lord in prayer
Can we find a *friend* so *faithful*
Who will all our sorrows share?
Jesus knows our ev'ry weakness
Take it to the Lord in prayer

Jesus experienced how it felt to be *poor* and *lonely. St. Luke* mentioned this in his 9:58. Here, *Jesus* told a man who wanted to follow *Him*, wherever he went, that "Foxes have holes and birds of the air have nests; but the *Son of Man* hath not where to lay *His* head." His *greatest sense of loneliness* came *as He was crucified* when *He* cried out to *His Heavenly Father*, "*My God, My God* why have *You* forsaken *Me*."

Jesus, at times, personally *felt great sorrow and grief. John* related this emotion in his 11:35. He *testified that "Jesus wept"* at the tomb of *His* friend Lazarus. In another instance, in the garden of Gethsemane, shortly before *His* crucifixion, it is recorded by *Jesus's* disciple, *Matthew*, that, *He (Jesus)* took with *Him* (to the Mount of Olives) Peter and the two sons of Zebedee, and began to be sorrowful and very heavy…and saith *He* unto them, "*My* soul is exceeding sorrowful, even unto death: tarry ye here, and watch with *Me*." And *He* went a little farther and fell on *His* face, and prayed, saying, "O *My Father*, if it be possible, let this cup pass from *Me*: nevertheless not as *I* will, but as *Thou* wilt" 26:37–39). This same event was recorded in *Luke* 22:44, which reads as follows: "And being in an <u>*agony*</u>, <u>*He*</u> prayed more earnestly: and <u>*His sweat*</u> was as it were <u>*great drops of blood*</u> falling down to the ground."

Because <u>*Jesus*</u> personally felt that <u>*He Himself needed comfort*</u> at times, <u>*He is able to understand*</u> that many *other people at times need it* as well. During *His* ministry here on earth, <u>His</u> great compassion for those who suffered from leprosy, blindness, demon possession, loneliness, confusion, anxiety, crippling diseases, and other adversities, is recorded in Matthew 9:36. It reads as follows: "But when *He [Jesus] saw the multitudes, He* was moved with compassion on them, because they fainted, and were scattered abroad, *as sheep having no shepherd.*"

In another book, that of *St. Luke*, it speaks of *Jesus's* compassion for a woman who had lost her son to death. It is related in 7:13 that "when *the Lord* saw her, *He had compassion* on her, and said, 'Weep not.' And *He* came and touched the bier: and they that bare him stood still. And *He* said, 'Young man, *I* say unto thee, Arise.' And <u>*he that was dead sat up*</u>, and began to speak. And *He* delivered him to his mother."

No pain that we can share
But *He* has felt its smart;
All forms of human grief and care
Have pierced *that tender heart.*

—Henry W. Baker

Because *Jesus Himself craved compassion, He understands our need for compassion and comfort. He* said, "Let not your heart be troubled:

ye believe in *God*, believe also in *Me*... *I* will pray the *Father*, and *He* shall give you *another Comforter*, that *He* may abide with you *forever*; even the *Spirit of truth*; whom the world cannot receive, because it seeth *Him* not, neither knoweth *Him*: but ye know *Him*; for *He* dwelleth with you, and shall be in you. *I* will not leave you comfortless: **I will come to you**" (previously stated, when we are believers and trust in *Him*, *Jesus*, *He* comes to us, and gives us *His* "joy" and "peace").

There is an added purpose to our being comforted by the *Holy Spirit*. As St. Paul explained in his *second letter to the Corinthians*, "Blessed be *God*...the *God* of all *comfort*; who *comforteth us* in all our tribulation, *that we may* be *able* to *comfort them* which are *in* any *trouble*, by the comfort wherewith we ourselves are comforted of *God*." *We can truly be <u>God's instrument</u> for blessing other people, thereby increasing their "joy".*

Creator Spirit, by *Whose* aid
The world's foundations first were laid,
Come, visit ev'ry humble mind;
Come, ***<u>pour your joys</u> on humankind***;
From sin and sorrow set us free;
May we Your living temples be.

—Rabanus Maurus

Chapter 14

For unto us a *child* is born, unto us a *son* is given: and
the government shall be upon *his* shoulder: and *his
name* shall be called <u>Wonderful</u>, <u>Counsellor</u>, <u>The Mighty
God</u>, <u>The Everlasting Father</u>, <u>The Prince of Peace</u>.

—Isaiah 9:6

In order for **Jesus** to be **true God, He needed to be omniscient
(all-knowing)**, filled with **perfect wisdom, holy** (completely without
sin), **omnipotent (all-powerful), (present everywhere), and perfectly loving**.

As *evidence* of being *omniscient (all-knowing)*, *Jesus Himself predicted* many things, most of which *already came to pass*. For example,
it is recorded in the *New Testament* in *Luke* 21:20 and 24 that *He
predicted that Jerusalem* would be *destroyed* and that *the Jews* would
become *captured* and *taken* from their homeland *to other nations*.
These are *His* actual words: "And when ye shall see *Jerusalem* com-
passed with armies, then know that the desolation thereof is nigh…
and they shall fall by the edge of the sword, and shall be led away
captive into all nations: and *Jerusalem* shall be trodden down of the
Gentiles, *until the times of the Gentiles be fulfilled*." (The Jewish people were brought back and became the nation of Israel in 1948.)

In *Luke* 19:28 and 41–44, it is told that "*He* went before,
ascending up to *Jerusalem*…and when *He* was come near, *He* beheld
the city, and *wept over it*, saying, If *thou hadst known*, even thou,
at least in this thy day, *the things which belong unto thy* <u>peace</u>! *But
now they are hid from thine eyes*. For the days shall come upon thee,
that thine enemies shall cast a trench about thee, and compass thee

"

round, and keep thee in on every side, and shall lay thee even with the ground, and thy children within thee; and *they shall not leave in thee one stone upon another*; because thou knewest not the time of thy visitation." **This prediction came true when Jerusalem was besieged by the armies of Titus and Vespasian.*

Shortly before *He* was arrested and crucified, *Jesus made a prediction about Peter* (one of *His* most avid and faithful followers), which is recorded in *Luke* 22:34 as "And *He* said, '*I* tell thee, Peter, *the cock shall not crow this day, before that thou shalt thrice deny that thou knowest Me.*'" **His* prediction came true as was later stated in *Luke* 22:54–62 as follows: "Then they took *Him [Jesus]*, and led *Him* into the high priest's house. And Peter followed afar off. And when they had kindled a fire in the midst of the hall, and were set down together, Peter sat down among them. But a certain maid beheld him as he sat by the fire, and earnestly looked upon him, and said, 'This man was also with *Him*' *[Jesus]*. And *he denied Him [Jesus]*, saying, 'Woman I know *Him* not.' And after a little while another saw him, and said, 'Thou art also of them.' And *Peter said, 'Man I am not'*. And about the space of one hour after, another confidently affirmed, saying, 'Of a truth this fellow also was with *Him [Jesus]*: for he is a Galilean'. And *Peter said, 'Man, I know not what thou sayest.*' And, immediately, while he yet spake, *the cock crew.* And the *Lord* turned, and looked upon Peter. And Peter remembered the *Word* of the *Lord*, how *He had said* unto him, '*Before the cock crow, thou shalt deny Me thrice.*' And Peter went out, and wept bitterly."

Jesus predicted He would be betrayed by one of His disciples as recorded in *Luke* 22:21. There it states that *He said*, "But, behold, *the hand of him that betrayeth Me is with Me on the table.*" St. *Matthew* also recorded the *Lord's prophecy* of betrayal when he stated in his book, in 26:1–2, "And it came to pass, when *Jesus* had finished all these sayings, *He* said unto *His* disciples, 'Ye know that after 2 days is the feast of the Passover, and the *Son of Man is betrayed to be crucified.*"

Jesus even predicted His own death and resurrection, which is recorded in **Mark** 8:31. Here it is revealed, "Then **He [Jesus]** began to teach them that the **Son of Man** must undergo **great suffering**, and be **rejected** by the elders, and the scribes, and be **killed**, and *after three days rise again*." Again, in the book of **John**, it states in 12:32, "And *I*, when *I* am lifted up from the earth, will draw all people to *Myself*." The following verse declares, "**He** said this to indicate the kind of death **He** was to die [*crucifixion*, the Roman practice of execution by nailing the victim's hands and feet to an elevated tree]." In **Matthew** 26:32, **Jesus** said, "But after *I* am risen again, *I* will go before you into Galilee." You will recall that even **King David** (in the **Old Testament**) *was aware that Jesus would not remain in the grave. David* declared in **Psalm** 16:10, *"Neither wilt thou suffer thine Holy One to see corruption (decay after death)."*

Jesus also predicted His Ascension into heaven when *He* stated (as recorded in *John* 7:33), "Yet a little while am *I* with you, and then *I* go unto *Him* that sent *Me*" (unto *His Heavenly Father*).

Another prediction by Jesus was that some of His followers would be persecuted and even be put to death. Jesus said, "They shall lay their hands on you, and persecute you, delivering you up to the synagogues, and into prisons, being brought before kings and rulers for *My* name's sake…and some of you shall they cause to be put to death" (recorded in *Luke* 21:12 and 16). *This did, indeed, happen* to some of his most avid disciples. According to *Scripture, Stephen* was the *first to be martyred* for the faith (recorded in *Acts* 7:58–60). He was <u>stoned</u> to death. Recorded in the booklet *Thy Kingdom Come* are more examples of many of the original twelve disciples who dedicated their lives to their *divine Master* and lost their lives, rather than deny *Jesus* as *Messiah*. One of these was *James*. In that same booklet, it is recorded that "*early historians testify* to the high repute in which he was held by non-Christians and Christians alike. A man of exemplary holiness, he was popularly known as *'The Just.'*" Choosing martyrdom rather than deny *Jesus*, he calmly prayed for those who *beat him to death*. Scholars deduce that *Bartholomew* and *Nathanael* were the same person, and traditionally, he is said to have died a *martyr in Armenia* after making many converts. *Simon the Zealot* is closely linked with the apostle *Jude*. A western tradition holds that he preached the gospel in *Egypt* before joining *Jude* in *Persia, where both were martyred*."

The method of **Simon Peter's death** *was* **foretold by Jesus** as recorded in **John** 21:18. **He** told **Peter**, "When thou shalt be old, thou shalt stretch forth thy hands, and another shall gird thee, and carry thee whither thou wouldest not." The following verse of that chapter related, "This spake **He**, signifying by what death **Simon Peter** should glorify **God**." Peter was, indeed, **crucified [with hands outstretched]**, *****just as was predicted by Christ**. Sadly, <u>persecution</u> [sometimes leading to martyrdom] has been the *plight of many a faithful Christian throughout the centuries, *just as Jesus had predicted.* "*Tortured for Christ*" is a *true account* of the *horrific experiences of a Romanian pastor* during his *fourteen-year confinement in Communist prisons. Pastor Richard Wurmbrand* describes in graphic detail the physical and mental sufferings that He endured, starting in 1948 when He was arrested by Communists who had taken over *Romania*. Given one slice of bread a week, eating dirty soup every day, placed in bitterly cold cells or repeatedly placed in icebox "refrigerator cells" to within minutes of death, placed in handcuffs with sharp nails on the inside, forced to stand for endless hours in wooden boxes only slightly larger than his body (with dozens of razor-sharp nails driven into every side of the box so that any movement would inflict painful wounds), beaten, being carved in a dozen places, being burned and cut, suffering four broken vertebrae in his back and other broken bones, and forced to sit for seventeen hours a day being brainwashed with chants of "Communism is good! Christianity is stupid!"

By the grace of God, he miraculously not only *lived* to write about it but also *founded a network of offices that provide relief to the families of imprisoned Christians* in Islamic nations, Communist Vietnam, China, and other countries where Christians are even *now* being <u>*severely* *persecuted*</u> for their faith in *Jesus Christ*.

Many of these followers were so *totally convinced that Jesus was the promised Messiah* that they actually <u>*gave up their very lives*</u> for *bringing the Gospel (good news of salvation in Jesus Christ) to everyone they possibly could. (Dr. D. James Kennedy)*

Jesus has also *predicted* what will happen in the days preceding *the end* of the *world* and what will happen at the end of the world as we know it. *St. Matthew*, in his twenty-fourth chapter, recorded the *prophecy of Jesus* in several terms as follows: "*As the days of Noah were, so shall also the coming of the Son of Man be*…iniquity [*sinfulness*] shall abound…this *gospel of Jesus Christ* shall be <u>preached</u> in *all the world* as a witness unto all nations…ye shall see the *abomination of desolation*, spoken of by *Daniel the prophet, stand in the holy place* [*Daniel*, at the end of his book, *predicted* that there would come *a man* who *would disregard the God* of his fathers and *honor a (false) god* whom his fathers knew not, *pollute* the *sanctuary* of strength, take away the daily sacrifice, and *exalt* and magnify *himself* as being divine]…there shall arise *false Christs* and *false prophets*, and shall *show great signs* and wonders and *deceive many*… There will be *great hatred and persecution of the believers in Christ… Many shall betray one another*, and hate one another…and then shall be *great tribulation, such as was not since the beginning* of the world to this time…except those days should be shortened, there should no flesh be saved: but for the elect's sake those days shall be shortened…immediately after, shall the *sun be darkened*, and the *moon shall not give her light*, and the *stars shall fall* from heaven, and the *powers of the heavens* shall be *shaken*: and then shall *appear the <u>sign</u>* of the *Son of Man* in heaven: and then shall *all the tribes* of the earth *mourn*, and they shall see the *Son of Man* coming in the *clouds* of heaven with *power* and *great glory*…and *He* shall send *His angels* with a *great sound of a <u>trumpet</u>*, and they shall *gather together his elect (His followers-all the Christians)* from the four winds, from one end of heaven to the other (from *Matthew* 24)."

Jesus also declared that *He* would ultimately be the *"**Judge**" of all people*. It is recorded in *Matthew* 25 that *He* stated, "When the *Son of Man* shall come in *His* **Glory**, and all the holy angels with *Him*, then shall *He* sit upon the throne of *His* glory:

And before *Him* shall be gathered all nations: and *He shall separate them* one from another, as a shepherd divideth his sheep from the goats: and *He shall set t*he sheep *[His followers]* on His <u>right</u> hand.

The Sheep

But the goats *[the <u>unbelievers</u>] on the <u>left</u>.* Then shall the *King* say unto them on *His* right hand, 'come, ye blessed of *My Father, inherit the kingdom prepared for you…*for *I* was an hungred, and ye gave *Me* meat: *I* was thirsty, and ye gave *Me* drink etc…inasmuch *as ye did it unto one of the least of these My brethren, ye have done it unto Me.* Then *He shall say also unto them on the left hand, 'Depart from Me, ye cursed, into everlasting (forever) fire [punishment]…*inasmuch as <u>*ye did it* **not** *to one of the least of these, ye did it* **not** *to Me.*</u>'

The goats

Before *His* ascension into heaven, *Jesus told His followers, 'In My Father's house (heaven) are many mansions: I* go to *prepare* a *place* for *you…*and *I* will come again, and receive you unto *Myself,* that *where I am, there ye may be also'"* (*John* 14:2).

Jesus also declared that *His* coming would be at a time when we least expect it. *He* said, "Know this: if the owner of the house had known at what hour the thief was coming, he would not have let his house be broken into. *You also must be ready, for the Son of Man is coming at an unexpected hour*" (*Luke* 12:39–40). ARE YOU READY?

Jesus is described in Luke 2, **as being "filled with wisdom: and the grace of God was upon Him."** He **is also described in Colossians** as **one "in whom are hid all the treasures of wisdom and knowledge"** (**Colossians** 2:3). **His omniscient (all-knowing) nature and perfect wisdom enable Him to know our every need and what is ultimately best for us. If we completely trust Him and have a loving, personal relationship with Him, we can be assured that He will meet those needs and grant us great peace and joy in this life, and the greatest possible Peace and Joy in the life to come.**

St. Paul wrote, "But my **God** shall supply all your need according to **His** riches in glory by **Christ Jesus**." (**Philippians** 4:19)

Blessed Assurance, *Jesus* is mine!
O what a foretaste of glory divine!
Heir of salvation, purchase of God,
Born of *His Spirit*, washed in *His blood*.

—Fanny Crosby

Chapter 15

There was *no other good enough*
To pay the price of sin
He only could unlock the gate
Of heav'n and let us in

—Cecil F. Alexander

In order to be divine, Jesus needed to be completely without sin. Being holy, *He could perfectly obey the Heavenly Father's laws.* In fact, *He did this in our stead,* because we are unable to do so. In chapter 5 of the apostle Paul's *second letter to the Corinthian church,* he says the following: "*He* made *Him* to be sin for us, *Who* knew no sin; that we might be made the *righteousness* of *God* in *Him.*"

In another letter, this time to the **Hebrews**, St. Paul wrote, "For we do not have a high priest **Who** is unable to sympathize with our weaknesses, but we have **One Who has been tempted** in every way, just as we are—**yet was without sin**" (**Hebrews** 4:15). This was demonstrated in the gospel where it spoke of the temptations that the devil made to *Jesus (Matthew 4:1*–11*).* The evil one was defeated by **Jesus** by **His using of the Word of God in the Holy Scriptures, Jesus** *never* sinned. This was also substantiated in *1 John 3:5*, which states, "In **Him** is no sin." When **Jesus** asked **His** original twelve disciples whether they wished to go away from **Him** (desert **Him**), **Simon Peter** told **Jesus**, '**Lord**, to whom can we go? **You have the words of eternal life.** We have come to believe and know that **You are the Holy One of God**'" (**John** 6:68–69). **Only a completely holy, sinless Son of God could keep the Law for us and die in our stead in order to perfectly heal our broken relationship with God and**

satisfy God the Father's requirements for being our Savior from eternal punishment. No sinful human being could have done it. <u>Only</u> **Jesus Christ** met that perfect qualification.

> And on *His* thorn-crowned head
> And on *His sinless soul*
> *Our sins* in all their guilt *were laid*
> *That He might make us whole.*

> —Henry W. Baker

Chapter 16

Be still, my soul;
The waves and winds still know
His voice who ruled them
While *He* dwelt below

—Catharina Amalia Dorothea von Schlegel

In order to be <u>divine</u>, Jesus needed to be omnipotent (all-powerful as only God is). Evidence of this occurs in the *Old Testament* and in the *New Testament.* You will recall that King David said, "Neither wilt *thou* suffer *thine Holy One* to see corruption" (prophecy and proclamation of *Jesus's* <u>divine power</u> in *His* future resurrection from the dead).

Jesus's great power was constantly being *demonstrated.* First was *His power* in the form of *His miraculous birth.* Then there was <u>*power in His Words,*</u> the *many miracles* that *He* performed while *He* was on earth, in the *forgiving of sins,* and in *His rising from the dead.* It is recorded in *Matthew* 7 that after *Jesus* preached the "Sermon on the Mount," the people were astonished at *His doctrine: for He taught them as one having authority* and not as the scribes. St. *Luke* recorded in his fourth chapter that "*He [Jesus]* came down to Capernaum, a city of Galilee, and taught them on the Sabbath days. And *they were astonished* at *His* doctrine: for *His Word* was *with power.*"

Jesus Himself proclaimed *His power* over *life* and *death. John* recorded, in his tenth chapter, a time when *Jesus* had said, "*I* lay down *My* life in order to take it up again. No-one takes it from *Me*, but *I* lay it down of *My* own accord. *I* have power to lay it down, and *I* have power to take it up again. *I* have received this command from *My Father.*" At another time, *He* declared *His* divine nature and power when *He proclaimed* to all those present, "*<u>All power is given unto Me in heaven and on earth</u>*" (*Matthew* 28:18). This means that *He* is so powerful that *He has control over absolutely everything!*

Jesus has the power to forgive sins. This was demonstrated when **He** said unto the sick of the palsy, "Son, thy sins be forgiven thee." A few minutes later, **He** told the unbelieving scribes sitting there, "Whether is it easier to say to the sick of the palsy, Thy sins be forgiven thee; or to say, Arise, and take up thy bed, and walk? But that **<u>ye may know</u>** that the **Son of Man** hath power on earth to forgive sins, [**He** saith to the sick of the palsy], **I** say unto thee, Arise, and take up thy bed, and go thy way into thine house." And immediately he arose, took up the bed, and went forth before them all; in so much that they were **all amazed**, and **glorified God**, saying, 'We never saw it on this fashion'" (**Mark** 2).

St. Peter confirmed *Jesus's* authority and power when He spoke of *Christ* in the following manner: "*Jesus Christ… Who* is gone into heaven, and is on the right hand of *God*; angels and authorities and powers being made subject unto *Him*" (*1 Peter* 3).

There are **many examples** of **Jesus's** divine power, and they were **witnessed** by **many** others. They were **recorded by His disciples** and appear in all four of the **Gospels of the New Testament**: **Matthew**, **Mark**, **Luke**, and **John**. In performing miracles, *Jesus* not only "manifested *His* glory" but **also showed that He is interested in the everyday events of our lives and has the <u>power</u> to help us in our adversities.** *His* very **first miracle** was at a **wedding** in the city of **Cana** in Galilee (**John** 2). **Jesus's mother,** *Mary,* had told **Him** that there was **no longer any wine** and then **told the servants to do exactly what Jesus said**. The servants were told by **Jesus** to fill six pots with water, and **they (the servants) obeyed**, filling them up to the brim. *Jesus* then <u>changed</u> <u>the</u> <u>water</u> <u>into</u> <u>wine</u>. The ruler of the feast tasted the new wine and then commented, "Thou hast kept the good wine until now." According to Pastor Adrian Rodgers, **that event was rich in symbolism**. He said that in the *Holy Scriptures,*

wine happens to be the **symbol** for **joy**. Therefore, ***Jesus was trying to teach us that if we obey Him, our lives will be filled with*** many moments of "**joy**".

O I am my *Beloved's*
And my *Beloved's* mine!
He brings a poor vile sinner
Into *His "house of wine"* [joy]

—Anne Ross Cousin

In *Matthew 8*, there are *six separate miracles*! They are as follows: In verses 2 and 3, it is revealed that "there came a leper and worshiped *Him*, saying, '*Lord*, if *Thou* wilt, *Thou* canst make me clean.' And *Jesus* put forth *His* hand, and touched him, saying, '*I* will; be thou clean.' And immediately, his *leprosy* was *cleansed*."

In verses 5–7, and 13, *it testifies* that "when *Jesus* was entered into *Capernaum*, there came unto *Him* a *centurion*, beseeching *Him*, And saying, '*Lord*, my servant lieth at home sick of the palsy, grievously tormented.' And *Jesus* saith unto him, '*I* will come and heal him.' The centurion answered and said, '*Lord*, I am not worthy that *Thou* shouldst come under my roof. : but speak the *Word* only, and my servant shall be healed.' When *Jesus* heard it, *He* marvelled, and said to them that followed, '*Verily I* say unto you, *I* have not found *so great faith*, no, not in Israel…and *Jesus* said unto the centurion, 'Go thy way; and as *thou hast believed*, so be it done unto thee.' And his *servant was healed* in the *selfsame hour*."

Verses 14 and 15 tell of *another healing*. "And when *Jesus* was come into Peter's house, *He* saw Peter's wife's mother laid, and *sick of a fever*. And *He* touched her hand, and *the fever left her*: and she arose, and ministered unto them." *Matthew* documents in verse 16 and 17 that "when the even was come, they brought unto *Him* many that were possessed with devils: and *He cast out the spirits with His Word, and healed all that were sick: *that it might be fulfilled which was spoken by Esaias the prophet, saying, 'Himself took our infirmities and bare our sicknesses.'*"

Verses 24 through 27 describe *a terrible storm in which Jesus calmed the wind and waves by the power of His Words*. The verses reveal in graphic detail that "behold, there arose a great tempest in the sea, in so much that the ship was covered with the waves: but *He* was asleep. And *His* disciples came to *Him*, and awoke him, saying, 'Lord, save us: we perish.' And *He* saith unto them, 'Why are ye fearful, O ye of little faith?' Then *He* arose, and rebuked the winds and the sea; and there was a great calm. But the men marvelled, saying, 'What manner of man is this, that even the winds and the sea obey *Him*!'" *That particular miracle* has great significance in that it *demonstrated* that *Jesus* has *power* over all the *"storms"* that occur in our *lives* and can surely *help* us *"weather" those difficult times*. The following verses of that same chapter testify that *Jesus had power over devils who knew He was the Son of God and, as such, would have power over them. The testimony* is as follows: "There met *him* two possessed with devils, coming out of the tombs, exceeding fierce, so that no man might pass by that way. And, behold they cried out, saying, 'What have we to do with *Thee, Jesus, Thou Son of God?* Art *Thou* come hither to torment us before the time?' And there was a good way off from them a herd of many swine feeding, so the devils besought *Him* saying, 'If *Thou* cast us out, suffer us to go away into the herd of swine.' And *He* said unto them, 'Go.' And when they were come out, they went into the herd of swine: and, behold, the whole herd of swine ran violently down a steep place into the sea, and perished in the waters."

Another disciple, **John, testifies**, in his gospel in chapter 9, that **Jesus returned sight to a blind man**. He says, namely, "And as **Jesus** passed by, **He** saw a man which was blind from his birth… and **He** spat on the ground, and made clay of the spittle, and **He** anointed the eyes of the blind man with the clay, and said unto him, 'Go, wash in the pool of Siloam.' He went his way, therefore, and washed, and came seeing." According to world-famous theologian **Charles Stanley, that** particular **miracle** demonstrated not only **Jesus's power** but also **showed** us that **He came** to **open the eyes of the "spiritually blind"**—**giving them "His Light.**" Remember, as previously mentioned, that **Jesus said that He was the "Light of the World."** Another set of miracles was when *Jesus* walked **on water** to reach a boat, and ***He also caused His disciple Peter to walk on water toward Him***. As long as Peter focused his eyes on ***Jesus***, he stayed afloat, but as soon as he looked down at the water beneath him, he started to sink (***Matthew*** 14:28–33). This set of miracles has a point to it. Jesus ***was telling all of us that as long as we keep our focus on Him, instead of on <u>our</u> <u>circumstances</u>, we will be able to rise above our troubles, maintaining "joy" in our heart (because of the <u>strength</u> that He gives us)***. Some of the other miracles include the healing of a nobleman's son (***John*** 4), the ***<u>raising</u> of <u>Lazarus</u> from the <u>dead</u>*** (***John*** 11), and the feeding of five thousand people with only five loaves of bread and two fish (***John*** 6, ***Matthew*** 14, ***Mark*** 6, and ***Luke*** 9). The last of these demonstrates that ***Jesus is and gives "the Bread of Life" (life abundantly now and forever)***. In ***John*** 20:30–31, it is revealed that "***many other signs*** (miracles) ***truly did Jesus in the presence of His disciples, which are not written in this book: "But these are written, that ye might believe that Jesus is the Christ, the Son of God;*** and <u>that</u> <u>believing</u> <u>ye</u> <u>might</u> <u>have</u> <u>life</u> <u>forever</u> <u>through</u> <u>His</u> <u>name</u>."

"How Firm a Foundation"

"Fear not! <u>I</u> *AM* with you,
O be not dismayed,
For <u>I</u> *AM your God* and will still
Give you aid;
I'll strengthen you, help you,
And cause you to stand,
Upheld by *My* righteous,
Omnipotent *(all-powerful)* hand.

Because Jesus is all-powerful, He can give us all of the strength, "peace," comfort, and "joy" that we will ever need throughout the "storms" of life. He said, "Cast all your care upon ***Me***, and ***I*** will give you rest" (***1 Peter*** 5:7). The apostle Paul, in his letter from Rome to the early Christians in Ephesus, wrote, "Be strong in the ***Lord***, and in the <u>power</u> of ***His*** might" (***Ephesians*** 6: 10). **He** also wrote to the Christians in Philippi, "I can do all things through **Christ who** <u>strengthens</u> me" (**Philippians** 4:13). In the **Old Testament**, in the book of **Nehemiah**, it says, "The **"joy" <u>of the Lord</u>** is your <u>strength</u>." *To follow Him and have a wonderful loving relationship with Him is to be on the <u>pathway</u> which ultimately leads us to "peace" and to "joy" in this life and the life to come.*

Every day the *Lord Himself* is near me
With a special mercy for each hour;
All my cares *He* fain would bear, and cheer me,
He whose name is *Counsellor* and *Pow'r*.

The protection of *His* child and treasure
Is a charge that on *Himself He* laid;
"As thy days, thy <u>strength</u> shall be in measure,"
This the pledge to me *He* made.

—Lina Sandell Berg (Based on *Deuteronomy* 33:25)

Chapter 17

Into the *heart of Jesus*, deeper and deeper I go,
Seeking to know the reason why *He* should love me so-
Why *He* should stoop to lift me up from the miry clay,
Saving my soul, making me whole, Tho I had wandered away.

—Oswald J. Smith

Jesus needed to have perfect love in order to be divine. In the third chapter of St. Paul's letter to the ***Ephesians***, Paul writes, "And I pray that you, being rooted and established in love, may have power…to grasp how **<u>wide</u>** and **<u>long</u>** and **<u>high</u>** and **<u>deep</u>** *is the love of Christ*, and to know this love that surpasses knowledge…" According to *1 John* 4:8, ***"God is Love."*** Therefore, ***being God, Jesus was love itself***, sent into this world in human form. In ***His*** acts of miraculous power, ***He*** not only gave evidence of ***His*** divine nature but also showed ***His perfect*** all-encompassing *love* for *others* and for ***His Heavenly Father. Jesus demonstrated that perfect love by serving others*** in the form of ***His many miracles and works of compassion.*** At one point, ***He*** even washed ***His*** disciples' feet (***John*** 13:12). ***He*** said, "Greater love hath no man than this, that a man lay down ***his*** life for his friends" (***John*** 15:13.) Both ***Matthew*** (in his chapter 20) and Mark (in his chapter 10) ***testified*** to having heard ***Jesus*** state that ***He would, "give His life a ransom for many." He*** did just that at ***His*** crucifixion! Timothy declared the same in his first letter when he declared, "***Christ Jesus***…gave ***Himself*** a ransom for all" (***1 Timothy*** 2:6). In ***John*** 10, it is recorded that ***Jesus*** said, "***I*** lay down ***My*** life, that ***I*** might take it again. No man taketh it from ***Me***, but ***I*** lay it down of *Myself*. ***I*** have the power to lay it down, and ***I*** have the power to take it again. This commandment have *I* received of ***My Father***." The fact that *Jesus* was willing to lay down *His* very life in obedience to *His Father* and <u>**for us**</u> is the very greatest of all testimonies to *His* <u>perfect divine love</u>. ***He*** is all powerful. ***He*** could easily have foiled the plans of those who were out to kill ***Him***. ***He*** instead showed <u>***His*** <u>greatest love</u> by surrendering ***His*** own will to that of ***His Heavenly Father***, saying, "Not as *I* will, but as ***Thou*** wilt" (***Matthew*** 26:39 and ***Mark*** 14:36). In so doing, ***He*** suffered during ***His*** crucifixion in **constant excruciating pain** in order to save us from <u>eternal torment</u>. I sincerely pray that we all repent of our sins, accept *His* forgiveness and *His* sacrifice, try very hard to obey *Him*, and deeply trust *Him* for that salvation.

Into the *love* of *Jesus* deeper and deeper I go,
Praising the *One who* brought me out of my sin and woe;
And thru eternal ages <u>gratefully</u> I shall sing,
"O how ***He loved***! O how ***He loved***!
Jesus, my ***Lord*** and my ***King***!

—Oswald J. Smith

Chapter 18

Jesus said, "For where two or three are gathered together in *My* name, "*I AM*" there in the midst of them."

—*Matthew* 18:20

In order to be divine, Jesus needed to be omnipresent (present everywhere). Jesus was present in the beginning of the world as *John* wrote in his chapter 1, "In the beginning was the *Word [Jesus]* and the *Word* was with *God*, and the *Word was God…*and the *Word was made flesh* and dwelt among us, and we beheld *His glory*, the glory as of the *only begotten of the Father*." Jesus also said, "Verily, verily [truly], *I* say unto you, *before Abraham was, 'I AM'*" (*John* 8:58). The "*I AM*" *refers to God's name as previously stated by God in Exodus* 3.

Jesus was, in effect, saying here that He is truly God Himself (the second personality of God). When He was speaking with Nicodemus, **Jesus** revealed, "No one has ascended to heaven but **He** who came down from heaven, that is, the **Son of Man** who is in heaven" (**John** 3:13). **He** was saying that **He** was initially in heaven, came down from heaven, and later ascended back to heaven. As **He** ascended into heaven, **He** said to **His** disciples, "Lo, "**I AM**" with you alway, even unto the end of the world" (**Matthew** 28:20). **He** also said, "**I** will never leave thee nor forsake thee" (**Hebrews** 13:5). **If we are true believers in *Him*, *He* (*Jesus*) is constantly in us and with us in order to help us in all circumstances.**

Be still, my soul; your *God* will undertake
To guide the future as *He* has the past.
Your hope, your confidence let nothing shake;
All now mysterious shall be bright at last.

—Katharina von Schlegel

Chapter 19

Part A

Jesus Christ said, "I AM" the Door: <u>by Me</u> if
any man enter in, <u>he</u> <u>shall</u> <u>be</u> <u>saved</u>."

—*John* 10: 9

There are <u>many</u> instances in the Old Testament in which God, in His <u>perfect</u> <u>wisdom</u>, <u>illustrated</u> the "<u>way</u>" <u>to</u> <u>salvation</u>. For example, as illustrated in *Exodus*, just as Moses led the people of Israel to their promised land (Canaan), *Jesus* leads us to our promised land (heaven). Also, during the Great Flood (*Genesis* 7), there was *only one door* leading into Noah's Ark (the only place of salvation from death). There is **<u>only one door</u>** <u>*leading to salvation from eternal death. (torment)*</u> **<u>Jesus Christ</u>** <u>*said,*</u> **<u>"I AM"</u>** <u>*the*</u> **<u>Door."</u>**

Part B

Behold the *Lamb of God*, which taketh away the sin of the world.
— ***John*** 1:29

Another **Old Testament** illustration of the way to salvation occurred in **Genesis** 22, where Abraham, following **God's** instruction, went to <u>**Mount Moriah**</u>, took a ram (a male sheep) and offered it up as a blood sacrifice. Similarly, ***the Heavenly Father offered up His Son, the Lamb of God, Jesus Christ, as a blood sacrifice so that trusting Him, we could have our sins forgiven and be saved from eternal punishment.*** According to **Steve Cohen, Director of The Apple of His Eye evangelism to the Jewish people**, ***this*** supreme sacrifice **even** occurred **on the** <u>same</u> mountain range!

GLORY

From the mount of *glory*
To the hill of shame
Counted with the guilty
Bearing all <u>our</u> blame.

He was bruised and beaten,
Pierced to take <u>our</u> pain.
Wounded and afflicted,
Dying for <u>our</u> gain.

Chosen by the *Father*,
His dear *Son* alone;
Flowing with the *Spirit*,
God can now be known.

Trust *Him* as your *Savior*
He your *Friend*, indeed.
He will always hold you.
Satisfy your need.

Glory, praise and blessing
To the *Lamb* we sing
Honor and adore *Him*
Crown *Him* as our *King*.

—Pastor Ferdinand O. Bahr
c. 1997

Part C

The *God* of Abr'ham praise,
Whose all-sufficient grace
Shall *guide* me all my pilgrim days
In all my ways.
He deigns to call me *friend*;
He calls *Himself* my *God*.
And *He* shall save me
To the end
Through ***Jesus's*** blood.

Just as Abraham's sacrifice points to Jesus, the Messiah, so does the Passover. God had commanded the Israelites to place the blood of a lamb on their doorpost so that they could be saved from death. The lamb had to be without a single blemish just as Jesus was without the blemish of sin. By God's design, it was in the very hour that thousands of lambs were being slain for the Passover celebration, that the true Passover Lamb died (Jesus Christ) to save us from eternal death in "hell" (pp. 232, *The Murder of Jesus* by evangelist John F. MacArthur Jr.). *In the temple in Jerusalem,* there was a *thick veil or curtain which separated the holy of holies from the congregation.* The significance of this was that the *people's sins separated them from God.* The *Bible* testifies in both *Matthew* 27:51 and *Mark* 15:37–38 that "***Jesus, when He had cried again with a loud voice, yielded up the ghost***, *(died) He* gave up *His* spirit. *And behold, the veil of the temple was rent (torn) in two from the top to the bottom.*" This was explained in *Hebrews* 9:12 where it says, <u>*"By His own blood He entered once into the holy place, having obtained eternal redemption for us."*</u>

When the veil was rent in two pieces, it meant that *God* had removed the barrier and established a *(New Covenant-***New Testament***)*, a <u>new relationship</u> with us in which He would remember our sins no more. (Remember that this came from the *Old Testament* in *Jeremiah* 31:34). *God* was, in effect, saying, *"My Son has removed this veil and eliminated the need for it, through a single, perfect, once-for-all sacrifice that cleanses the redeemed from their sins forever"* (pp. 231 and 232).

David Brickner, Executive Director of **Jews for Jesus**, made a truly beautiful statement regarding this in his April of 2005 newsletter. He proclaimed, "When the **prophet <u>John the Baptist</u>** saw **Jesus**, he announced, 'Behold the **Lamb of God** who takes away the sin of the world.' ***Just as the blood of the lamb saved the Jewish people in Egypt from the plague of death, so Jesus is <u>our Lamb</u>. Through His sacrifice, <u>Jesus</u> is <u>our Savior</u> if we are willing, in a sense, to put His blood on the doorposts of our hearts.***"

Part D

<u>Guide</u> me, O Thou great Redeemer
Pilgrim through this barren land
I am weak, but *Thou* art mighty
Hold me with *Thy* pow'rful hand
Bread of Heaven, Bread of Heaven
Feed me till I want no more

—William Williams

In the **Old Testament**, in **Exodus**, there is *further symbolism concerning salvation*. Just as **God saved** the people of **Israel** from the **slavery** they suffered in Egypt, **God provided** a **way** to <u>**save us**</u> from the **slavery** of **sin**. Just as **God** had **provided bread** (manna) from **heaven** in order **to save** the children of Israel from death, **God provided** (from **heaven**) **Jesus**, who not only was born in **Bethlehem** (meaning **house** of **bread**) but also called *Himself* '**The Bread of Life.**" **He Himself** said, "Your fathers did eat manna in the wilderness…this is the **bread** which cometh down from heaven, that a man may eat thereof, and not die. *'I AM' the living bread* which came down *from heaven: if any man eat of this bread, he shall live forever: and the bread that I will give is "My flesh," which I will give for the life of the world*" (*John* 6:51).

Part E

Another illustration of the way to salvation is recorded in the Old Testament in Numbers 21. *Moses* was commanded by *God* to make a *fiery serpent* of brass and set it on a pole. He was told that if a serpent had bitten any man, *the man would live only if he looked up* and *beheld* the *serpent* of *brass*. Moses did as commanded, and the people who were saved were the ones who looked up at the brass serpent. In the *New Testament*, in *John* 4:14, it is recorded that *Jesus* said to *Nicodemus, "As Moses lifted up the serpent in the wilderness, even so must the Son of Man be lifted up: that whosoever believeth in Him should not perish, but have everlasting life."*

His wondrous works and ways
He made by *Moses* known,
But sent the world *His truth and grace*
By *His beloved Son.*

Part F

<u>*All the Way*</u> *my Savior* <u>*leads*</u> <u>*me*</u>
What have I to ask beside?

Can I doubt *His* tender mercy,
Who thru life has been *my Guide?*

Heav'nly peace, divinest comfort,
Here by faith in *Him* to dwell!
For I know, whate'er befall me,
Jesus doeth all things well.

—Fanny Crosby

In a recent radio broadcast called *Bible Tract Echoes*, **Bible** teacher and Director of **Bible** Tracts Inc., **Mark Smith**, spoke of how **Joseph** in the **Old Testament** (**Genesis** 37–50) ***was a true picture of the "Messiah" to come, Jesus.*** This picture pointed to the promise of a **Savior** to come. He said that first of all, ***Joseph*** was the **son of <u>his father's old age</u> just as Jesus is the Son** of **His** Heavenly <u>**Father**</u>, who has existed <u>***from of old***</u>. Secondly, ***Joseph was <u>especially loved by his father</u>***, to the point of adorning him with a coat of many colors. **God**, the **Father**, <u>**especially loved**</u> **His Son Jesus** to the point of adorning **Him** at **His** birth with a special star and a special song (by the angels of heaven). Other ***parallels*** are as follows:

Both Joseph and Jesus had more than one name. Joseph, as an adult, was given a second name by the pharaoh of Egypt. That name was called Zaphnathpaaneah. *Jesus's* second name was Christ. *Both Joseph and Jesus were hated for their words. Joseph* was hated by his brothers for relating to them his dreams of *sovereignty. Jesus* was hated by people because *He* told them to repent and *He* said that *He* was a *king (a sovereign). Both were betrayed for money* (pieces of silver). *Joseph* was *sold* into slavery, and *Jesus* was *sold* into being arrested. *Both were uniquely opposed to evil and turned away from it. Joseph* refused to sin against his master, Potiphar, (by rejecting the seduction attempt by Potiphar's wife). *Jesus* refused to sin, even when severely tempted by the devil in the wilderness (*Matthew* 4), on the pinnacle of the temple, and on the high mountain. *Both were brutally slandered and suffered much. Neither one of them complained, but instead ministered to those around them. Both won the respect of a Gentile. Joseph* won the respect of the pharaoh of Egypt, and *Jesus* won the respect of the Roman governor Pontius Pilate. *They both forgave the people who hurt them so deeply.* *Joseph* forgave his brothers, and *Jesus* forgave those who nailed *Him* to the crucifixion tree. *Both were exalted to positions of sovereignty.* *Joseph* became the second in command ruler over the people of Egypt, and *Jesus* rules the world from on high. Finally, *God sent both to* save people. *Joseph* saved his people (the Israelites) from hunger and starvation and physical death by giving them grain for *bread*, and *Jesus* was sent by *God the Father* to save *His* people (the Israelites) from physical hunger when *He miraculously fed large groups* of people *with bread*, and *most importantly, He was sent to save all people (Jews and Gentiles) from eternal death by giving them the "Bread of Life" (Himself)* (*John* 6:35).

Guide me, O thou great *Redeemer*

Pilgrim through this barren land.
I am weak but Thou art mighty
Hold me with Thy powerful hand.
Bread of heaven, Bread of heaven
Feed me till I want no more;
Feed me till I want no more.

Chapter 20

A certain woman in those days spoke to *Jesus*, saying, "I know that *Messias* cometh, which is called *Christ*: when *He* is come, *He* will tell us all things." *Jesus* answered, "*I* that speak unto thee *AM He*."

—*John* 4:25–26

There are many other passages in the **Scriptures** pointing to **Jesus** as our **Messiah** (our **Savior**) Some of these are the following:

> **God** so loved the world, that **He** gave **His** only begotten **Son**, that whosoever believeth in **Him** should not perish, but have everlasting life. (*John* 3:16)

> For *God* sent not *His Son* into the world to condemn the world; but that the world through *Him* might be saved. *He* that believeth on *Him* is not condemned; but he that believeth <u>not</u> is condemned already, because he hath <u>not</u> believed in the name of the only begotten *Son of God*." (*John* 3: 17–18)

> *Jesus, Himself,* said, "If any man serve *Me*, him will *My Father* honour." (*John* 12:26)

In **John** 3:36, we are told that **John the Baptist**, in addressing a *Jewish audience*, proclaimed, **"He that believeth on the Son hath**

everlasting life: and he that believeth <u>not</u> the Son shall not see life; but the wrath of God abideth on him."

Romans 8:1–4 reveals the following:

> *There is therefore now <u>no</u> condemnation to them which are in Christ Jesus*, who walk not after the flesh, but after the *Spirit*. For the law of the *Spirit of life in Christ Jesus* hath made me free from the law of sin and death. For what the law could not do, in that it was weak through the flesh, *God* sending *His own Son* in the likeness of sinful flesh, and for sin, condemned sin in the flesh: That the righteousness of the law might be fulfilled in us, who walk not after the flesh, but after the *Spirit*.

In *Matthew* 10:33, it is stated that *Jesus* said," Whosoever shall deny *Me* before men, him will *I* also deny before *My Father which* is in heaven."

In *Acts* 4:10–12, we are told by the apostle (missionary) *Peter* the following:

> Be it known unto you all, and to all the people of Israel, that by the name of **Jesus Christ** of Nazareth, **whom** ye crucified, **whom God** *(the Father)* **raised** from the **dead**, even by **Him** doth this man stand here before you whole. This is the **stone** which was set at nought of you builders, which is become the **head** of the **corner**, *(the cornerstone or foundation). Neither is there salvation in any other: for there is none other name under* heaven, given among men, *whereby we must be saved.*

Jesus said to the woman at the well, "Whosoever drinketh of this water, shall thirst again, but whosoever drinketh of the water that *I* shall give him, shall never thirst; …shall be in him a well of water springing up into *everlasting life*." (***John*** 4: 13–14)

For the *Son of Man* came not to be served but to *give His life* a *ransom* for *many*. (*Hebrews* 5:45)

This is **love**: not that we loved **God**, but that **He loved us and sent His Son as an <u>atoning sacrifice</u> for our sins**. Dear friends, since **God** so loved us, we ought to **love one another**. **(1 John 4:10–12)**

For the **Son of Man is come to seek and to save that which was lost.** (**Luke** 19:10)

Ye know that *He [Jesus <u>Christ</u>] was manifested to take away our sins; and in Him is <u>no sin</u>*." (*1 John* 3: 5)

Jesus said, "He that liveth and believeth in <u>Me</u> will never die" [will have eternal life]. (***John*** 11:26)

Therefore being *justified* by *faith*, we have "<u>peace</u>" <u>*with*</u> <u>*God*</u> *through* our *Lord Jesus Christ*. (*Romans* 5:1)

Believe on the **Lord Jesus Christ**, and **<u>thou</u>** shalt be **<u>saved</u> <u>*(from the punishment of sin)*</u>**. (*Acts* 16:31)

Jesus said, *"I AM"* the *"Way"*, the *"Truth"*, and the *"Life."* <u>No-one</u> *comes to the Father except through <u>Me</u>."* (*John* 14:6)

"<u>You</u> Are the "Way," through You <u>Alone</u>"

You are the **Way**, the **Truth**, the **Life**;
Grant us that **Way** to know,
That **Truth** to keep, that **Life** to win,
Whose *Joys* eternal flow.

Chapter 21

How to have a Personal Relationship with *Jesus Christ*

I never fully came to the realization that it was possible to have a very _intimate_ and _loving relationship with Jesus_ until I started writing this book. I found that each day, as I either read or heard *Scripture* passages or hymns. I felt as though there was some *mysterious force* leading me to use these words and also leading me to other passages dealing with the same topic, giving me new incite on how to present the material. It seemed _magical_. I can truly say that *I now know and understand* what it is like to be led by the Holy Spirit. That feeling blossomed into a _spiritual_ *"daily walk with Jesus."*

Throughout each day, in my _thought life_, I periodically find myself _"talking to Jesus,"_ primarily _thanking Him_ for each new blessing as it occurs and _following His advice or commands_ as _He_ presents them to me. I often recognize that I am getting advice from _Him_ when a _thought_ comes to me, _in a command format_. For example, my thought is not, "Maybe I should do this," or "I wonder if I should do this," but rather, _"Do this,"_ or "I should do this." I am always careful to be sure that the action is _something Jesus would do_, so as to avoid any disobedient actions or thoughts that the devil could be sending me. I have found that, _many times, I would receive_ some kind of _"blessing" within minutes_ of doing something that I knew would please _Him_. One particular time, I did something to help someone, and a few minutes later, after walking into a store, I immediately spotted a vase that perfectly matched my set of earthenware dishes that I had been collecting for some time. The inscription said, _"Bless Our Home."_ Another time, I had just written an order for some more Christian tracts, and within minutes, I found the pearl that I had lost out of my ring over a week before. One other time, I had just put an evangelism sign on my car, and right after that, I found a calligraphy pen that I had lost months before. I see that _Jesus_ is blessing other Christians in this manner as well (adding _"joy"_ to their life).

Always include _Jesus_ in every thought and action of your day, never forgetting that _He_ knows you and every aspect of your life intimately and is there right beside you, _guiding_ you in every decision that you make. If you are not sure what course to take, talk to _Him_ in _prayer_ and ask for _His_ help. Martin Luther once made a very profound statement regarding prayer. He said, _"Oh, if I could only pray the way this dog watches the meat! All his thoughts are concentrated on the piece of meat. Otherwise, he has no thought, wish, or hope."_ Regarding prayer, _Jesus taught_ the disciples _how to pray_ when they asked _Him_ how to pray. _Jesus_ taught them what is widely known as _"The Lord's Prayer"_ located in the _New Testament_ in _Matthew_ 6:9–13 and that we can also _pray_ to _Jesus Himself. He_ intercedes for us. In other words, _He pleads with His Heavenly Father for us_. It never pays to worry about anything if you are a true Christian because God already has a plan for our life, and we can and should trust _Him_ completely. *We may have to* <u>wait</u> for that plan to be fulfilled, but that plan will ultimately do so. It says in *Romans* 8:28, "*And we know* that *all things work together for good* to *them* who *love God*, to *them* who are *called according to His purpose.*"

Loving God means constant *worship* and *praise* in words or songs, communicating often with *Him* by *prayer*, abundant *thankfulness*, *faithfulness*, and *obedience*. *God's Word* also tells us, *"Delight thyself also in the Lord; and He shall give thee the desires of thine heart"* (*Psalm* 37:4). I, myself, can testify to that. I had to wait thirteen years to have my wish fulfilled. (between ages twenty-four and thirty-seven). I needed *to learn many important things* during that time of *waiting*, including *proper communication* and *humility* instead of being prideful, but in the end, *my wish for a <u>Christian</u> <u>husband</u> was wonderfully fulfilled by the Lord.* In the fourth chapter of the letter the apostle Paul sent to the Christians in Philippi, he wrote, "In everything by prayer and supplication with thanksgiving let your requests be made known unto *God*. And the *"<u>Peace of God</u>,"* which passeth all understanding shall keep your hearts and minds through *Christ Jesus.*"

Lord, we *thank you* for each day.
May it please you in every way.
Glory, honor, thanks and praise
Be unto *Thee* for endless days.

—Bob Rothwell

Many times, I have seen *how magnificently Jesus makes all things come together or "match."* One such instance was when I had purchased a set of earrings during one winter, and, months later, discovered that the earrings "mysteriously matched" a new logo that the church had placed on T-shirts, advertising the prayer labyrinth on our church property. Another instance was when I was creating a scene on a poster for my child evangelism class. The lesson was about the transfiguration of *Jesus*. I was trying to depict a city during a glorious sunset and, in my mind, was wondering how I could possibly draw a mountain on the scene in light of my being the world's worst artist. While using a rub-on bird sticker, the entire set of stickers adhered to the sky on the poster, and some parts of those stickers stayed on the page permanently. They were birdhouses! I was horrified! But suddenly, I knew how to create the mountains! I simply cut out the bad stickers in such a way as to reveal the brown parts of the poster and then pasted the rest of the sky above it. *Jesus* had used my *mistake to show me exactly how to make the mountains!* Each time I see these things happening, it *causes me to love Jesus even more, because in His being so concerned with even the minute details of my life, He makes me feel so loved and cherished by Him.*

It would be impossible to feel a *personal, loving attachment* without the process of really *getting to know Jesus*. You wouldn't have a best friend or spouse unless you knew him or her very well, would you? In the same manner, it is vital that we *learn all about Jesus (our very best friend) and what He stands for*. In addition to seeing how *He works in our lives* each and every day, *we must hear, read, or sing the words of Jesus*, either by going to church, listening to Christian radio and television, attending *Bible* studies, or doing personal *Bible* reading. *Jesus*, in nourishing us by *His* words, *strengthens us* emotionally and spiritually. *His* words provide *a moral compass* for us to follow in our everyday living and decision-making. All these things *need to be done on an ongoing basis*. You can't get to really know *Him* unless *you talk to Him in prayer, sing to Him, listen to Him*, and *show* that you *love Him* by *obeying Him. He* said, "If ye love *Me*, keep *My* commandments" (*John* 14:15).

Jesus Lives! The Victory's Won

Jesus lives! For me *He* died;
Hence will I, to *Jesus* living,
Pure in heart and *act* abide,
Praise to *Him* and glory giving.
All I need *God* will dispense;
This shall be my confidence.

Jesus's commandments were ***given*** to prevent us from having a ***lack*** of ***"joy"*** (emotional and physical pain) and a ***lack*** of ***"peace"*** (anxiety). If you are living a self-centered ungodly life, you are rebelling against ***Him*** and all that ***He*** stands for. ***He*** will not bless that life or you. If, however, you ***obey Him*** in all that you do, ***He*** will always prove that ***He*** is your constant ***best friend. If you do what pleases Him, He will always give you "His best."*** The "best" that ***He*** gives ***is a life (here and forever) filled with "peace" and "joy."*** No one could ever ask for more!

> What a *friend* we have in *Jesus*
> All our sins and griefs to bear
> What a privilege to carry
> Ev'rything to *God* in *prayer*
> *O what peace we often forfeit*
> O what *needless pain* we bear
> All because we do not carry
> Ev'rything to *God* in *prayer*

Chapter 22

Be filled with the *Spirit…giving thanks always for all things unto God* and the *Father* in the name of our *Lord Jesus Christ.*

—*Ephesians* 5: 18 and 20

Part A

****Jesus Christ first loved each and every one of us so much that He was willing to suffer an* agonizing and *brutal death so that we would have the chance to be saved from an eternity of torment.* This should inspire us to be truly *thankful to Him and love Him back* in such a way that we are continually motivated to *do what pleases Him* and makes *Him* "smile." In the *Old Testament*, in *Deuteronomy,* it is recorded *what will happen if we obey God.* It states, "And it shall come to pass, if thou shalt hearken diligently unto the voice of the *Lord thy God,* to observe and to do all his commandments which I command thee this day, that ****the Lord thy God will set thee* on *high above all nations of the earth: and all these blessings* ("joy") *shall come on thee, and overtake thee."*

"<u>*Blessed*</u> shalt thou be *in the <u>city</u>,* and blessed shalt thou be *in the <u>field</u>. <u>Blessed</u>* shall be the *fruit of thy body (children),* and the fruit of thy <u>ground</u>, and the fruit of thy <u>cattle</u>, the <u>increase</u> of thy kine (cattle), and the *flocks* of thy sheep. Blessed shall be thy basket and thy store. Blessed shalt thou be when thou comest in, and blessed shalt thou be when thou goest out."

We've already demonstrated that *Jesus is God,* and as *God, Jesus made the statement, "If ye love Me, keep My commandments"* (*John* 14:15). *He* made only <u>*three basic commandments*</u>. The *first* is to "*love the Lord, thy God with all thy heart, and with all thy soul, and with all thy mind"* (*Matthew* 22:37). This encompasses the first four of the *Ten Commandments* given by *God* as listed in *Exodus* 20. The *second* is to *"love thy neighbor as thyself"* (*Matthew* 22:39). This encompasses the last six of the *Ten Commandments*. The *third* is to *"go and make disciples of all nations"* (*Matthew* 28:19). This last commandment may even be considered *an extension of loving God and loving others* with whom we come in contact. If we don't make sure that others have heard the *Scripture* verses relating to the only way to heaven as voiced by *Jesus*, it means that we don't love *God* enough to obey *Him*, and we don't love our neighbor enough to try and save him or her from a miserable life here on earth, and an even more miserable eternity. That is breaking not one but all three of the commandments of *Jesus*. *Jesus's* disciple John witnessed the following declaration by *Jesus* to *His* followers, located in *John* 13:35, namely, that *"by this shall all men know that ye are My disciples, if ye have love one to another."* We should *pray* that *Jesus* would *ignite* in our *hearts* the *powerful flame* of *His perfect love* so that we can *truly love* and *help* other *people. A big part of that love is sharing the gospel (good news of salvation in Jesus) with everyone we meet. We can also pray for the unsaved and for the success of the missionaries and give money to the missionary effort.*

Go Forth in Radiant Joy

The time is short;
Oh hear the *Master's call*
<u>Decide</u> <u>today</u>
To Follow *Him* through all.

"Go forth in radiant *joy*
Plant seeds of *love*.
<u>*Proclaim My Word,*</u>
And *I* will build *My Church*.
It Will Endure!"

The fields are white
The harvest is at hand
Do not delay
Press on at *His command*

"Go forth in radiant *joy*
Plant seeds of *love*.
<u>*Proclaim My Word,*</u>
And I will build My Church
It Will Endure!"

<u>*Witness for Christ*</u>
That dying souls may live.
With *Spirit's* power
The Kingdom message give.

Reach out in <u>Love</u>
That empty hearts be filled
Reach out in <u>Peace</u>
That troubled hearts be stilled

"Go forth in radiant *joy*,
Plant seeds of *love*.
<u>*Proclaim My Word,*</u>
And *I will build My Church.*
IT WILL ENDURE!"

—Pastor Ferdinand O. Bahr
c.1985

Concerning helping to bring little children to faith in *Jesus*, there is an international organization called *Child Evangelism Fellowship* which provides *free training to volunteers* who wish to help in the various *"Good News Clubs,"* which are being *held after school at public schools* in this country and abroad. These are perfectly legal and are *similar to Sunday school classes. Instruction* is given to the children

If you cannot speak like angels,
If you cannot preach like *Paul*,
<u>You</u> can <u>tell</u> the <u>love</u> <u>of</u> <u>Jesus</u>,
<u>You</u> can say <u>He</u> <u>died</u> <u>for</u> <u>all</u>.

If you cannot rouse the wicked
With the judgment's dread alarms,
<u>You</u> can <u>lead</u> the little <u>children</u>
<u>To</u> the <u>Savior's</u> <u>waiting</u> <u>arms</u>.

Let none hear you idly saying,
"There is nothing I can do,"
While the multitudes are dying
And the *Master* calls for you.

Take the task **He** gives you **gladly**,
Let *His* work your pleasure be;
Answer quickly when *He* calleth,
"<u>Here</u> <u>am</u> <u>I</u>, <u>send</u> <u>me</u>, <u>send</u> <u>me</u>!"

—Daniel March

Part B

Therefore **if any man be in Christ, he is <u>a</u> <u>new</u> <u>creature</u>**: old things are passed away;_behold, all things are become new.

—*2 Corinthians* 5:17

Go to those who <u>suffer</u>,
Deeds of <u>kindness</u> share.

Healing and *forgiveness*,
Help their burdens bear.

Share the love of Jesus.
Let His Heart be known.
His your hands and voices,
His the mercy shown.

—by Pastor Ferdinand O. Bahr

By being in a very special, personal relationship with Jesus, we are changed spiritually, and it shows in our behavior and actions. Other people should be able to "behold" *how different our lives are compared to those of unbelievers.* We should be **"living letters"** to all those around us. How are we different? We are moved to exhibit *Christlike Behavior* and to be *Christ's ambassadors.* This is evident in the words of *Peter* (one of *Christ's* disciples) *in his first epistle*, 2:21. We read there, "For even hereunto were ye called: because *Christ* also suffered for us, *leaving us an example*, that ye should follow *His* steps."

Jesus Christ came to earth as a humble servant. He exhibited that humble servanthood by going so far as to wash *His* disciples' feet (*John* 13:12). After performing that most humble act, *He* declared, "*I* have given you an example, that ye should do as *I* have done to you." In other words, *He wants us to humbly* (not pridefully) *and joyfully serve others* (our friends, spouses, children, all other family members, and all of those other people who are in need). Serving others means *helping other people who are in need*, physically, emotionally, and spiritually. Some people, especially the disabled and depressed, are helped by simply listening to them (by phone or in person). *Good and proper communication* is a vital part of getting along with people, *especially in* marriage. That type of communication involves using the same *encouraging words* as talking to *Jesus.* Those words are *full of praise, truthfulness, thankfulness*, and *love, not criticism and dominance. These concepts would prevent many divorces, problems with children, and all types of crime.*

In This Union *I* Have Joined You

Husband and wife,
Now, *My* children,
Live together
As heirs of *life*:

Each the other's **<u>gladness sharing</u>**,
Each the other's burdens bearing,
Now *My* children, live together
As heirs of life.

The first chapter of the book of *James* (from the *New Testament*) clarifies the concept of <u>service</u> to others. James says, *"Faith, if it hath not works, is dead... I will show thee my faith by my <u>works</u>."* He added, *"Be doers of the Word, and not merely hearers...doers who act-they will be blessed in their doing." Jesus* even said that, "If ye know these things, *happy ("joyful") are ye if ye do them"* (*John* 13:17). In *Revelation* 22:7, this is reiterated as it says, *"Blessed is he that keepeth the sayings of the prophecy of this book."*

If we are Christlike, we will obtain an added benefit—*"happiness"* and *"joy"* in the process. St. Paul wrote about the importance of *humble servanthood* in his epistle to the *Philippians* 2. It reads as follows: "Let this mind be in you, which was also in *Christ Jesus: who, being in the form of God,* thought it not robbery to be equal with *God:* but made *Himself* of no reputation, and took upon *Him the form of a servant,* and was *made in the likeness of men:* and being found in fashion as a man, *He humbled Himself, and became obedient unto death...*wherefore *God also hath highly exalted Him, and given Him a name which is above every name: that at the name of Jesus every knee should bow,* of things in heaven, and things in earth, and things under the earth; and that **every tongue should confess that Jesus Christ is Lord, to the glory of God the Father."*

St. Paul further states in his fifth chapter, "Be subject one to another, and be clothed with *humility: for God resisteth the proud, and giveth grace to the humble." Christ wants us to conform to His image, to be like Him—*<u>not</u> <u>selfish</u>, but <u>full</u> of <u>humility</u>, of <u>compassion</u>, of <u>love</u>, and of genuine concern for other people's physical, emotional, and spiritual needs *(provide help for them in as many ways as possible)*. "For whom *He* did foreknow, He also did predestinate to be conformed to the image of *His Son*" (from St. Paul's letter to the *Romans*, in 8:28–29).

Pastor John H. Kieschnick, in the book entitled *The Best Is Yet to Come*, made some beautifully profound statements regarding **service to Christ**. One of them is that "we are naïve to think that we can simply add *Jesus* to our existing set of desires and pursuits. *He* doesn't want to be an addition to our lives. ***He wants to be in the absolute center, where His interests become our interests, where what breaks His heart breaks our heart, and where what thrills Him thrills us***." The other statement is, "God wants our best efforts, not our afterthoughts. He doesn't want us to use a few scraps of time between 'really important' things. He wants us to use *some* of ***our best time*** to ***think*** about, ***pray*** about, and ***plan our*** "joyful" ***service*** so we can be as effective as possible. When we pray, we pray fervently; when we sing, we sing with gusto; ***when we serve, we want it to touch people and change lives***."

We should spend our life being a blessing to other people, and in so doing, we will obtain joy as a wonderful side effect.

More like Jesus would I be, Let my *Savior* dwell in me;
Fill my soul with *peace* and *love*, make me *gentle* as a dove;
More like *Jesus* while I go, pilgrim in this world below;
Poor in spirit would I be; let my *Savior* dwell in me.

—Fanny Crosby

Part C

O *Master*, let me walk with *Thee*
In lowly paths of service free

Tell me *Thy* secret—help me *bear*
The strain of toil, the fret of care.

—Washington Gladden

It follows that *in order to be a* truly <u>joyful</u> and <u>peaceful</u> <u>follower of Jesus Christ</u>, it is necessary that I make *Jesus Christ* the *Lord* and *Master of my life, not make myself master of my life. Jesus Himself* declared, "Ye call *Me Master* and *Lord*: and ye say well; for so *'I AM'*" (*John* 13). *He* also said, "No man can serve two masters: for either he will hate the one, and love the other; or else he will hold to the one, and despise the other. *You are either for Jesus Christ or you are against Him.* A good *illustration* of our relationship to *Jesus* is that of a "<u>Lord</u> of the *Manor*" in the *feudal system (from long ago).*"

As our **<u>Lord</u>, *Jesus is our Supreme authority***, but **He** is also the one who **takes care of us** and our **needs**. Because **He** is our **Lord** and **Master**, it is **our job** to **obey Him, serve Him, and follow where He leads and guides us**. There is a passage in **Psalm** 37 that tells of a **great <u>promise</u> that God gives to us**. It states, **"Delight thyself in the Lord; and He shall give thee the desires of thine heart"** **(<u>great joy</u>)**. As **God, He has infinite wisdom**, and as such, **He** will lead us in the <u>correct pathway</u> through this life, that which **leads to our greatest good and most abundant blessings**. **Jesus** said, "*I* am come that they might have **life**, and that they might have it more abundantly" (**John** 10:10). In **Proverbs** 3, the **Lord** tells us, "**Trust** in the **Lord with all thine heart**; and lean not unto thine own understanding. In all thy ways acknowledge **Him**, and **He shall direct thy <u>paths</u>**." We need to **completely surrender our lives to Him**. Someone told me once that the letters forming the word *Bible* could mean **"basic instructions before leaving earth."** That means that <u>all</u> of **<u>our</u> decisions** in our earthly life should **<u>not</u>** be **<u>made</u> <u>based</u> <u>on</u>** our own understanding, but on **the wisdom of God** found in the **Holy Scriptures**, especially in the books **Proverbs, Exodus**, and **Deuteronomy** (where **God's Ten Commandments** are listed), and in the entire **New Testament** books. In **Proverbs** 23:4, **God** tells us, "Cease from thine own wisdom." An example of **God's wisdom** is **found in Deuteronomy** 18. Here **God has warned us against certain spiritual dangers**. He states, "There shall not be found among you anyone who…practices **witchcraft, or a soothsayer, or one who interprets omens, or a sorcerer, or one who conjures spells, or a medium, or a spiritist, or one who calls up the dead**." **(<u>the</u> <u>devil</u> <u>can</u> <u>imitate</u> <u>their</u> <u>voices</u>)** These things **are** *part of the kingdom of the "prince of darkness"—the devil. Jesus* spoke of ***Satan (the devil)*** as "a ***liar*** and the father of it" (***John*** 8:44). Satan is ***also called "the destroyer" (1 Corinthians 10:10) and a "murderer"*** from the beginning (*John* 8:44). If you follow the devil and his ways, he will destroy both your earthly life and your life after death. In ***Ephesians*** 6, St. Paul warns us, "***Put on the whole armour of God, that ye may be able to stand against the wiles of the devil.*** For we wrestle …against principalities, against powers, against the rulers of the darkness of this world, against spiritual wickedness in high places." The devil is not omniscient (all-knowing) as ***God*** is. ***Only God knows the future.*** However, ***the devil is very knowledge-able***, very ***powerful***, and very ***clever***. He was ***originally an angel*** who was ***so proud*** that he ***rebelled against God*** and was ***thrown out of heaven***, together with some other angels who followed him (***Revelation*** 12:9). Therefore, he ***can even appear as a beautiful angel of light*** (***2 Corinthians*** 11:14) or even imitate the voice of your loved one who has died. He hates *God*, and he ***wants to keep you*** from *God*, rob ***you*** of "peace" and "joy" and *ultimately* to make ***you*** go to "hell". (after your physical death)

The *Bible* is filled with <u>*Godly Wisdom.*</u> For example, it has instructed us <u>regarding</u> *marriage* in the book of *2 Corinthians* 6:14, where it says, "*Be ye <u>not</u> unequally <u>yoked</u> <u>together</u> <u>with</u> <u>unbelievers</u>*: for what fellowship hath righteousness with unrighteousness? And what communion hath light with darkness?" In other words, a *Christian* should <u>*not marry*</u> an <u>*unbeliever*</u> *if he or she wants to have a joyful marriage.* The book of *Proverbs* contains a host of *wise sayings*. How about *Proverbs* 16:20, where it says, "He that handleth a matter wisely shall find good: and *whoso trusteth in the Lord, happy [joyful] is he.*" Again, in *Proverbs* 144:15, it reveals, "*Happy* is *that people, whose God* is the *Lord.*" Also, in *Proverbs* 23:21, it declares, "For the *drunkard* and the *glutton* shall come to *poverty,*" or *Proverbs* 6:32 where *God* says, "Whoso committeth <u>adultery</u> *with a woman lacketh understanding: he that doeth it destroyeth his own soul.*"

Some *other wise sayings* are as follows: *Proverbs* 11:13 declares, "A talebearer revealeth secrets: but he that is of a faithful spirit con-cealeth the matter." *Proverbs* 11:28 proclaims, "He that trusteth in his riches shall fall: but *the righteous shall flourish* as a branch." *Proverbs* 14:29 says, "He that is slow to wrath is of great understanding." Along those same lines is *Proverbs* 15:1: "A soft answer turneth away wrath: but grievous words stir up anger." And again in that same chapter, in verse 18, "A wrathful man stirreth up strife: but *he that is slow to anger appeaseth strife.*" *Proverbs* 22:24: "*Make no friendship with an angry man*; and with a furious man thou shalt not go."

Otherwise sayings from *God* are *Proverbs* 22:6: "Train up a child in the way he should go: and when he is old, he will not depart from it." *Proverbs* 19:17 declares, "He that hath pity upon the poor lendeth unto the *Lord*; and *that which he hath given will He pay him again.*" *Proverbs* 12:10: "A righteous man regardeth the life of his beast." *Proverbs* 16:18: "Pride goeth before destruction, and an haughty spirit before a fall." *1 Peter* 5:5: "Be clothed with *humility*: for *God* resisteth the proud, and giveth grace to the humble." *Proverbs* 19:5: "*A false witness shall not be unpunished*, and he that speaketh lies shall not escape." *Proverbs* 28:13: "He that covereth his sins shall not prosper: but whoso *confesseth* and *forsaketh them* shall have *mercy.*" *Proverbs* 3:5: "*Trust* in the *Lord* with all thine heart; and lean not unto thine own understanding. In all thy ways acknowledge *Him*, and <u>*He*</u> <u>shall direct</u> <u>thy</u> <u>Paths.</u>"

To go against God's commands leads to trouble! We do <u>not</u> get "*God's* <u>best</u>" for our lives when we don't obey *Him*. As was mentioned before, *God's* commandments *are meant to* <u>protect</u> *us* from great *physical and emotional* <u>pain</u>. I wish so much that that statement would have been taught and really emphasized in schools throughout the ages and that it would be taught now, being extremely helpful now and in the future. We read in *Psalm* 5:12, "For *You, O Lord*, will *bless the righteous*; With favor *You* will surround him as with a shield." *We may have to "Wait" on the Lord*, as it says in *Psalm* 27:14. The rest of that verse says, "Be of good courage, and *He* shall strengthen your heart." It isn't that we will never have troubles, but *God* will give us <u>*strength*</u> for those times and <u>in</u> <u>*His*</u> <u>own</u> <u>timing</u> will give us what, in *His* perfect wisdom, *He* knows is <u>*best*</u> for us. Great comfort is given to us in these words: *'Seek ye first the kingdom of God and His righ-*

teousness, and all these things shall be added unto you" (*Matthew* 6:33). This means that on any given day, *whenever possible,* our *first priority* should be to *praise* and *thank* our *Lord Jesus* and *do His work, then follow that with our other duties and plans. You will find that the day will go a lot smoother for you, with much less stress.* I can personally testify to the truth of that statement in my own life.

***It is <u>comforting</u> to know that "the *Lord* shall <u>guide</u> thee continually" (*Isaiah* 58:11). The <u>*pathway*</u> in which *Jesus* leads us will produce a sense of contentment, "peace", and "joy". When we are saved from eternal punishment by faith in *Jesus Christ* as our *Messiah,* the Scriptures say <u>that *Christ* actually lives in us</u>! In the apostle Paul's letter to the *Ephesians,* 3:17, he states, "That *Christ* may dwell in your hearts by faith." In Paul's letter to the *Galatians,* 2:20, he states that same thought when he says to them, "Nevertheless I live; yet not I, but *Christ* <u>liveth</u> <u>in</u> <u>me</u>; and the life I now live in the flesh *I live by the faith of the Son of God, who loved me, and gave Himself for me."*

As is recorded in **John** 15:11, **Jesus** said, "These things have I spoken unto you, that ***<u>My Joy might remain in you</u>**, and that **<u>your joy might be full</u>**." We actually get "Christ's Joy"! In that same book, in 17:13, it is related by **John** that **Jesus** also said, "And now come **I** to thee; and these things **I** speak in the world, so that they may have **My Joy** made complete in themselves." We can depend on those sayings of our **Lord** and what is written in **Nehemiah** 8, where it states, "The **<u>Joy of the Lord</u>** is **my <u>strength</u>**! **"True Joy"** can be summed up as the following: The J stands for **putting Jesus first** in our lives (giving **Him** first priority) the O stands for **<u>obeying Jesus</u>** and also for **putting <u>others</u> next** in priority, and the Y stands for you **(putting your needs and wants third)**.

Part D

When *Christ* lives in us, *He* will show us *His* purpose for our lives. When we follow that *purpose, there is no room or time for depression unless you are isolated from other people.* One of the greatest and most cunning of the *devil's weapons* is to make us feel sad, discouraged, and sorry for ourselves. *St. Peter, in his first epistle,* chapter 5, said that, "The devil, as a roaring lion, walketh about, seeking whom he may devour: whom *resist* stedfast in the faith…but the *God* of all *grace, Who* hath called us unto *His* eternal glory by *Christ Jesus,…*make you perfect, stablish, strengthen, settle you." We can call upon *God* to dispel the devil's plans for making us discouraged. *He* will *strengthen us. God* tells us in *James* 4:7 that we are to "resist the devil, and he will flee from you." This tells us that we ourselves can successfully resist the devil and his plans. We don't even need to ask *God* to help us resist Satan and all his works. The apostle Paul, in his *second letter to Timothy,* said, "For *God hath not given* us the spirit of *fear,* but of power, and of love, and of a *sound mind.*" When *Jesus* was tempted by the devil, *He* was the most vulnerable because at first, your body can get used to not eating, and you are not hungry anymore, but after forty days, *your body begins to consume itself* so that you start to get very, very hungry. Just as *Jesus overcame temptations of the devil by using the Word of God (Holy Scriptures),* we also can *overcome* the temptation to become *depressed* by the *same means.* Remember that verse in *Jeremiah* 29 about how *God has plans for us? Once we realize that Jesus has given us this earthly life in order for us to <u>fulfill</u> a <u>mission</u> for Him, and we <u>act</u> upon that mission, our depression will leave us because we will be very busy serving Him and other people who need our <u>help</u>.* George Eliot, the great English writer, had many quotes, but one of her best was, "What do we live for, if not to make life less difficult for each other." One of my friends, Doralene, sent me a marvelous quote, saying, "Pretend you're a star and poke a hole in someone's darkness." You can't help others if you don't get to meet them. *God* gave us others in order to not only help them, but to socialize with them, making both of us feel *"joyful." If we want to make ourselves available, we must communicate with and go where various <u>godly</u> people are.* For example, we could go to various social clubs or organizations such as book clubs, sport clubs, sewing or crafting classes, senior clubs, and last but not least, Christian church services and activities. Make plans ahead of time for the days ahead so that you will look forward to joining in on these activities. There will then be so much less time to think negative thoughts that make you feel sad and depressed.

The Gospel Shows the *Father's* Grace
It bears to all the tidings *glad*

And bids their hearts no more be sad;
The weary burdened souls it cheers
And banishes their guilty fears.

Before *He* left this earthly dwelling, ***Jesus*** promised, "I will pray the **Father**, and *He* shall give you another ***Comforter***, that *He* may abide with you forever; even the ***Spirit of truth* (the third personality of God)**; ***whom*** the world cannot receive, because it seeth *Him* not, neither knoweth *Him*: but ye know *Him*; for *He* dwelleth with you, and shall be in you. *I* will not leave you comfortless: ***I will come to you***" (***John*** 14:16–18). *We can "joyfully" *trust* in *Christ* to *guide us* through life and firmly *believe* what the Scriptures relate, namely, that *"all things work together for good to those who love God, to them who are called according to His purpose"* (*Romans* 8:28).

Perfect submission, *perfect delight*!
Visions of *rapture* now burst on my sight;
Angels descending bring from above
Echoes of *mercy*, whispers of *love*.

Perfect submission—all is at rest,
I in *my Savior* am happy and blest;
Watching and waiting, looking above,
Filled with *His* goodness, lost in *His* love.

—Fanny Crosby

Jesus answered, "These things have *I* spoken unto you, that **My Joy** might remain in you, and that ***your Joy*** might be full." (*John* 15:11)

Part E

Jesus said, "*My Peace* I give unto you."

—*John* 14:27

Jesus is the "Prince of Peace" predicted by the prophet Isaiah in his ninth chapter and referred to in his twenty-sixth chapter as follows: *"Thou wilt keep him in perfect peace, whose mind is stayed on Thee: because he trusteth in Thee"* (verse 3). Another verse which substantiates is in *1 Corinthians* 14:33, which states, "*God* is not the author of confusion, but of *peace.*" When *Jesus* lives in us, *He will give us not only "His joy," but also "His peace."* Therefore, we need not be anxious or afraid. *Christ's* disciple *John* conveyed this in two separate chapters of his gospel. The first of these in chapter 16:33, *John* related that *Christ* declared, "These things *I* have spoken unto you, *that in Me ye might have "Peace."* In the world ye shall have tribulation: but be of good cheer: *I* have overcome the world." Again, in *John* 14: 27, the *Lord Jesus said,* "*Peace* I leave with you, *"My Peace" I give unto you*: not as the world giveth, give I unto you. *Let not your heart be troubled, neither let it be afraid."*

In the apostle Paul's epistle to the **Hebrews**, the thirteenth chapter, Paul says, "**He [Jesus] hath said, 'I will *never* leave thee or forsake thee.'** So that we may boldly say, 'The Lord is **my Helper**, and I will not fear what man shall do unto me." ***In summary, *the **Pathway** to *Peace* and *Joy* is the **Pathway** that leads to *Jesus*, the **Savior** of our **souls**, our **Lord** and **Master**, our **Prince** of **Peace**, and our **Leader** through **this life** and the **eternal life** to come.

In ***hope that sends a shining ray
Far down the future's broad'ning way
that *only Thou canst give*
In *"peace"* With *Thee*, O *Master,*
Let me live.

—Washington Gladden

Chapter 23

Messianic Jews (those Jewish people who believe in Christ) and other believers in Christ have a strong feeling of "inner Peace." "Therefore being justified by faith, we have peace with God through our Lord Jesus Christ" (Romans 5:1). The Prince of Peace *predicted in *Isaiah 9:6* is *Jesus*, who promised, *"Peace I leave with you; My peace I give unto you:* not as the world giveth, give I unto you. Let not your heart be troubled, neither let it be afraid" (*John* 14:27). There is no reason why any Jewish person or Gentile couldn't experience and possess *"Jesus's peace"*—the promised *"peace of God which passes all understanding"* that "shall keep your hearts and minds through Christ Jesus" (*Philippians* 4:7) and the *peace* that fills one's heart, *knowing that he or she is forgiven and, therefore, saved from the punishment of sin.* That person will have the joy *of* knowing *that he or she will ultimately inherit eternal and everlasting life in heaven* where "there shall be no more death, neither sorrow, nor crying, neither shall there be any more pain" (Revelation 21:4.).

*Jesus, the Messiah, has paid the penalty of all our sins. ***You need to make the most important decision that you will ever make in your earthly life! And* you need to decide now, *because you could die at any time! You can either reject* Jesus *and face an eternity of absence from* God *and horrific punishment or* confess *your sins, truly* repent *of your sins (which involves living a new life), and* believe, obey *and* trust *in Jesus as your Messiah (Savior from the punishment of all your sins). ***Total surrender to your Loving Savior and total trust in Jesus is the "Pathway to peace and joy," and that Pathway will give you great Divine "peace" and "joy"* in this life and lead to your "Greatest Peace and Joy" *forevermore* in "*Heaven*."

Shalom (Peace)!

Dear Lord, Thank You for all the *hope* that fills our hearts, knowing that as *our Messiah, You* cherished us so much that *You* sacrificed *Yourself* in order to save us from the punishment of our sins. Help us to obtain freedom from guilt and anxiety so that we will feel *Your peace,* that "*peace* which passes all understanding," which we so vitally need. Kindle the dryness in our heart and ignite it, giving us the confidence to share this wonderful news with *others,* and show us the way to live a life of obedience and service to *You* and *others* because of the love and thankfulness we feel toward *You* and the knowledge that that kind of life will save us from much emotional, spiritual, and physical pain. Give us *"peace"* and *"joy"* in this life, looking forward to the *perfectly Peaceful and Joyful life* we will ultimately have *With You in Eternity in the next world. Amen.*

Shalom (Peace)!

> Like a river glorious is *God's Perfect Peace*
> Over all victorious in its bright increase
> *Perfect,* yet it floweth, fuller every day,
> *Perfect,* yet it groweth, deeper all the way.

—Frances Ridley Havergal

> May the *God* of *Hope* fill you with all <u>*Joy*</u> and <u>*Peace*</u>
> as you trust in *Him,* so that you may *overflow*
> with *Hope* by the <u>*Power*</u> of the *Holy Spirit.*

—*Romans* 15:13

Go Forth in Radiant Joy

> The time is short;
> O, hear the **Master's** call
> <u>Decide today</u>
> To **Follow Him** through all.

"Go forth in radiant Joy,
Plant seeds of *Love*.
<u>*Proclaim My Word,*</u>
And *I will build My Church.*
It Will Endure!"

The fields are white
The HARVEST is at hand
<u>DO NOT DELAY</u>
<u>Press on</u> at *His* Command

"Go forth in radiant <u>Joy,</u>
Plant seeds of *Love*.
<u>*Proclaim My Word,*</u>
And *I will build My Church.*
It Will Endure!"

<u>*Witness for Christ*</u>
That dying souls may LIVE.
With *Spirit's Power*
The <u>*Kingdom Message Give*</u>.

Reach out in <u>Love</u>
That empty hearts be filled
Reach out in <u>Peace</u>
That troubled hearts be stilled

"Go forth in radiant *Joy,*
Plant seeds of *Love*.
<u>*Proclaim My Word,*</u>
And <u>*I will build My Church*</u>.
IT WILL ENDURE!"

—Pastor Ferdinand O. Bahr
c. 1985

The Peace Prayer of St. Francis

Lord, make me an instrument of your <u>*Peace*</u>;
where there is hatred, *let me sow <u>Love</u>*;
where there is injury, *Pardon*;
where there is doubt, *Faith*;
where there is despair, *Hope*;
where there is darkness, *Light*;
where there is sadness, <u>*Joy*</u>.

Grant that I may not so much seek to be consoled
as *to Console*;
to be understood, as *to Understand*;
to be loved as to *Love*;
for *it is in giving that we receive,*
it is in pardoning that we are pardoned,
and *it is in dying that we are born to Eternal Life in heaven*
(if we are followers of Jesus Christ).

Amen.

References

Brickner, David. Director of Jews for Jesus Evangelism.org. April of 2005 news letter.

Brown, Michael L. 2000. *Jewish Objections to Christ*. Baker Books. A Division of Baker Book House Co. Grand Rapids, Michigan, 49516.

Currie, Robin and Stephen G. Hyslop. 2009. *The Letter and The Scroll; What Archaeology Tells Us about the Bible*. National Geographic Society.

Drosnin, Michael. 1997. *The Bible Code*. Simon and Schuster.

Franzmann, Werner H. 1989. *Bible History Commentary—New Testament. Volume 2*. WELS Board for Parish Education—2929 North Mayfair Road, Milwaukee, Wisconsin 53222. Moody Publishers.

Habermas, Gary R. 1996. *The Historical Jesus—Ancient Evidence for the Life of Christ*. College Press Publishing Company, Joplin, Missouri.

Hagin, Kenneth E. 1984. *I Believe in Visions*. Tulsa, OK: Faith Library Publications 1984, 6–7, rhema.org.

Holy Bible (King James Version).

Jewish Study Bible—Featuring the Jewish Publication Society (Tanakh translation). 1985, 1999. Oxford University Press.

Josephus, Flavius. *Antiquities of the Jews*.

Kennedy, Dr. D. James. 1997. *Skeptics Answered*. Multomah Books. A division of Random House Inc.

Kennedy, Dr. D. James. 2000. *Solving Bible Mysteries*. Thomas Nelson Inc.

Kieschnick, John H. 2006. *The Best Is Yet to Come*. Baxter Press, Friendswood, Texas.

MacArthur, John F. Jr. 2000. *The Murder of Jesus.* Word Publishing, a Thomas Nelson Company.

Madenberg, David R. with William J. Nelson. 1995. *Israel's Messiah?* Vantage Press.

McDowell, Josh. 1981. *Evidence That Demands a Verdict.* Here's Life Publishers.

Moody, Raymond A. Jr. 1975. *Life After Life.* Mockingbird Books Inc.

Muncaster, Ralph. 2002. *A Skeptic's Search for God.* Harvest House Publishers.

Palestinian Talmud

Patterson, Roger, 2007. "Evolution Exposed." Answers in Genesis. Answersingenesis.org.

Philips, Tom (Director of Catholics Serving the Lord). 2005. "Science Debunks Evolution."

Ross, Hugh. 1996. *Beyond the Cosmos.* Nav Press.

Spiro, Rabbi Ken. "Revolt of the Maccabees." History Resource article and class.

Stoner, Peter. 1963. *Science Speaks.* Moody Press.

Strobel Lee. 1998. *The Case for Christ.* Zondervan. Grand Rapids, Michigan 49530.

Tacitus, Cornelius. *The Annals.*

The Tanakh.

101 Scientific Facts and Foreknowledge. 2005. Eternal Productions.

The Voice of the Martyrs. 1940. *Wurmbrand: Tortured for Christ.* Hodder-Stoughton.

Thompson, Frank 1989. *New Chain-Reference Bible.* Third improved Edition (King James Version) containing Thompson's Original and Complete System of Bible Study with Chain References, etc. B.B. Kirkbride Bible Company.

Thy Kingdom Come. 1966. Gastonia, North Carolina: Good Will Publishers Inc.

Whitcomb, John C. Jr. and Henry M. Morris. 1961. *The Genesis Flood.* Baker Book House by the Presbyterian and Reformed Publishing Company.

Wiese, Bill. 2006. *23 Minutes in Hell.* Lake Mary, Florida: Charisma House.

Audiovisual Bibliography

Bahr, Pastor Ferdinand O, composer. 1997. *From the Mount of Glory.*
———1985. *Go Forth in Radiant Joy.*
Bartz, Pastor Paul. 2008. *Creation Moments, Inc.* Radio Broadcast PO Box 839, Foley, MN 56329. www.creationmoments.com or 800-422-4253.
DeShazo, Lynn. Composer of song. 2001. *Ancient Words.* Integrity Music,Inc.
Mortensen, Terry. *DVD.*
Rodgers Adrian. *Love Worth Finding.* Radio Broadcast August 7, 2006 and Love Worth Finding Ministries, Memphis, TN. http /www.lwf.org.
Rothwell, Robert, composer. *Lord We Thank You for Each Day.*
Stanley, Charles. *In Touch.* Radio Broadcast

About the Author

Amy E. Socha R.N has had a very unusual life. She attended Zion Lutheran Elementary School in Wausau, Wisconsin, and in 1961, she graduated as valedictorian of DC Everest High School in Schofield, Wisconsin. She then attended St. Mary's School of Nursing in Wausau, obtaining a Registered nurse diploma. Her career in that profession lasted for thirty-eight years. During the first thirty-five years of her eighty years of her life, *she overcame, <u>by God's grace</u>, many painful obstacles*, including a broken ankle and fibula, followed by the tragic death of both of her parents in a motor home fire in Florida. Directly through those circumstances, she met her wonderful husband of forty-three years. Arthur has been an elder at their church for forty-five years. Amy taught Sunday school for twenty-five years and also taught in Child Evangelism Fellowship classes for four years. Those classes are allowed to be held in public schools. Amy has been a member of the Evangelism board at church and also *distributes Christian tracts, from Bible Tracts Inc. and small New Testament Bibles in which passages regarding the "way" to eternal salvation are underlined in red*. She makes handmade greeting cards for church members, relatives, and friends (especially birthday cards). In addition, she makes and sells jewelry for missions. She and her husband have both been choir members, ushers, and shut-in callers. Amy is a true witness of how the many circumstances in a Christian's life are not coincidences, but are all part of a *<u>Master</u> <u>Plan</u> that God has for our life, a plan that ***leads to an abundance of blessings, especially "<u>Peace</u>" and "<u>Joy</u>".*